Build a Better B2B Business

*Winning Leadership
for Your
Business—to—Business
Company*

DAVID M. SHEDD

ISBN: 0615450946
ISBN-13: 9780615450940
Library of Congress Control Number: 2011902587

For my family,

I thank you for your love and support.

For my teams,

Job well done and thank you for the great ride
we have had together.

TABLE OF
CONTENTS

SECTION I - OVERVIEW

Chapter 1 – Introduction

> "Success or failure often depends on getting the
> fundamentals correct in an ambiguous world."
>
> *The Logic of Life*

- *Answers to the Final Exam*
- *What is this Book All About?*
- *The Outline of the Book*

Answers to the Final Exam

The final exam at the end of this book contains but two questions:

1. What are the three fundamentals of leading your winning business that require your uncompromising daily focus?

2. To build and improve your business, what three things do you intend to make yourself do, whether you want to do them or not?

The answer to the first question is as follows:

1. Do the right thing

2. Winning teamwork

3. Customer service

The answer to the second question depends on you. My advice is to choose the three ideas and concepts most important to your business. For best results, choose these ideas within 24 hours of finishing the book, write them down, focus relentlessly on executing, and get them done. Best of luck!

What is This Book About?

This book is all about focusing on the fundamentals to drive business success. To get back to question one, my contention is that to improve your business performance and be a successful business leader, you need to create a business culture and work environment in which you and every member of your organization believe, breathe, sweat and bleed:

1. Do the right thing

2. Winning teamwork

3. Customer service

These three fundamentals are pre-requisites for long term business success. But, they are not sufficient. Companies still need to innovate, to control costs, to continually improve processes and operations, to...

But, if these fundamentals are mastered, achieving your organization's further goals in innovation, cost control, process and operational improvement will be easier and, most importantly, will get done.

As always, having the goal to master these fundamentals is the easy part. The difficulty lies in actually doing it. I have written this book to explain these fundamentals and to give business leaders simple, concrete and doable ideas on how to build the culture of a winning business that ensures that the fundamentals are mastered.

You may ask whether this is just another business book. Yes, but with three twists.

The first twist is that I have spent the time leading in the trenches and can relate my experiences and suggestions that I and my team have put into practice on the ground. I have lived the story. As such, this differentiates from the more common type of business books. First, I am not a famous CEO writing about what made me successful and great. Second, although I read a lot of business books and even a bit of business scholarship, I am not a business thinker or intellectual with great ideas who has never put them into practice.

The second twist relates to stories. First of all, I love a good story (and a good quote) and feel that stories are vital parts of leadership communication. But, I believe in real stories not business fables. So, you will see plenty of real stories and anecdotes to illustrate the ideas and concepts.

The third twist relates to telling both the good and bad. Throughout my career, I have both succeeded and failed. As a person who believes in the value of candor and honesty, I will be telling you about the times and ways that I have succeeded and the occasions where I have failed.

What is the Outline of the Book?

In this Section I, I will tell you who I am and why am I writing this book. I will also discuss my target audience. In Section II, I will discuss my overall approach to business leadership, introduce the three fundamentals in slightly more detail, and discuss some of the basics of management and leadership. In Section III, IV, and V, I will

I have tried (or seen in action) the ideas and concepts that I present in this book. I have "eaten my own dog food."

discuss in more detail Do the Right Thing, Winning Teamwork, and Customer Service. Section VI concludes the book with a wrap-up and the Final Exam.

Chapter 2 – Background

"Make it as simple as possible, but no simpler."

Albert Einstein

- *My biography*
- *Why am I writing this book?*
- *The complexity trap*
- *The target audience*

My Biography

In this book, you will hear my voice throughout, both the good and the bad. And that is how it should be. Leadership is not about some abstract idea, and a leader is not some perfect person. A business leader is a person, an individual with a unique personality and set of skills, that helps others to win and leads his[1] business to success. As I will be your tour guide, it pays to know a little bit about me before we get started.

---

[1] Author's note: In order to reduce confusion, but at the risk of being politically incorrect, I will use the masculine pronouns throughout the book. Please rest assured that I am using them as placeholders for both male and female leaders.

My name is David Shedd. I graduated from Williams College in 1985 knowing that I wanted to go into business. So, I did what everybody interested in business during the height of yuppiedom does. I took the GMAT. And then, I went to teach math and European History to high school students in England.

After two years, I came back and dabbled at consulting before escaping to the Wharton School at the University of Pennsylvania to get an MBA. After graduating from Wharton, I now actually had a better idea of what I wanted to do. I wanted to run a business. So, I went to TRW, a diversified manufacturing company, as a management associate. I was in one of the then-popular corporate rotation programs where I got to see the company inside and out. I worked in each of the different businesses (Automotive Parts, Space and Defense, Information Systems and Services). I worked in all different types of business units (corporate headquarters, plants, division headquarters, and a German subsidiary). I worked at all different levels of the organization: at one point I worked on a special project for the CFO, so there was just one layer of management between the CEO and me; at another time, I worked on a project team where there were 12 levels of management between the CEO and me; and, I worked in every layer in between.

This experience at TRW was an eye-opener about how a corporation really works. And, it was an eye-opener about how accountability can falter and bureaucracy can form and pervade a company despite genuine effort on everyone's part to avoid bureaucracy.

The bureaucracy at TRW along with the Michigan weather led me on to Los Angeles, Oldcastle and the building materials industry in 1994. Back then, Oldcastle was growing rapidly and tremendously free-wheeling with little to no bureaucracy. I spent nearly 16 years there. For the first five, I was in business development, pursuing growth opportunities and acquisitions in the U.S., Mexico, and Canada. For the last 10½ years, I was a Division President.

As a Division President, I had full P&L (profit and loss) responsibility and full autonomy. I had between four and nine different business units or companies reporting to me. Each of these business units was run by either a General Manager or a President with full P&L responsibility and accountability. The business units ranged in size from $10M in annual sales all the way to $80M; with the average size of about $25M. I led a total of 19 of these companies in manufacturing, project management, services, and distribution. These businesses were located nationwide and in Quebec, Canada, and they served the telecommunications, infrastructure, building materials, environmental, utilities, government, alternative energy, and other industries.

I led many of these businesses through two nasty downturns (telecommunications collapse of 2001 – 2003 and the great recession of 2007 – 2009). My team and I were able to achieve three successful business transformations, turning around money losing businesses into highly profitable ones. We got the chance to start a business unit from scratch and grow it into a successful $25M division.

With the autonomy, my team and I made a lot of mistakes. But, we learned and did enough right to have significant success in growing the business, always exceeding budgets, and averaging a return on net assets of 35% from 2004 to 2009.

By the end of 2009, my division was the only one in the group to have exceeded budget for six years while actually increasing return on net assets in 2009 as the market collapsed. The reward for this performance was to be asked to leave the company and given a severance. Given the changed values and new goals for the company, the decision to ask me to leave was the right one as I will explain later.

For the last year, I have been consulting and advising small to middle-market B2B (business to business) clients on a wide variety of issues. But, mostly, I have been working with these companies to determine how to grow their businesses in the wake of the poor economic conditions. I have also been blogging on Winning B2B Leadership^SM at www.winningB2Bleadership.com.

In summary, I have had the opportunity to see business and business leadership from all sides.

Why Am I Writing This Book?

Throughout my time as Division President my job was to make my team better: to make my General Managers better General Managers; to make my sales team stronger; to make the operations and operations team more effective; to make all employees better employees. In doing this, I made use of my teaching background and taught numerous classes on business topics ranging from production and operational excellence to the fundamentals of sales and sales management to the basics of negotiation. Significantly, I initiated and personally taught for four years a three-day course called Precast University to more than 200 of the employees in my Division.

Through my leadership and this teaching experience, I have come to believe that most businesses can become more successful and most business leaders can become better leaders. But, this will not happen by doing more of the same things more efficiently and effectively. It will not happen by working harder.

In fact, I continue to be amazed at how hard business leaders and employees work and how dedicated they are. Businesses rarely fail due to a lack of effort. The teams in the failing businesses that we turned around were always working just as hard (if not even harder) than the teams in the winning businesses. Yet the businesses were failing nonetheless.

Business success will come, instead, by simplifying and focusing only on the important, the few key fundamentals that drive the success of the business.

Eliminate the complexity.

Eliminate all the useless effort.

It is better to do nothing than to do the wrong thing.

Simplify. Eliminate. Prioritize. Focus.

The Complexity Trap

With my goal of simplicity and focus, I may just be spitting into the wind. Everything and everyone in business, especially American business, drive business leaders and businesses towards greater and greater complexity and more and more work.

<u>Shooting for Perfection</u>

The first reason for greater complexity is the desire to be best in class in everything that a company does. We all know the words that are thrown about:

- World-Class
- Stretch Goals
- BHAG's (Big Hairy Audacious Goals)

As I have heard so often, "if you aim for the stars, you may just reach the moon."

Sometime skeptic that I am, I prefer: "if you aim for the stars you may just shoot yourself in the foot."

Why?

By shooting for the perfect 100% solution, the company undertakes a complex project or improvement initiative that it is often incapable of successfully completing. Using the analogy of baseball, you cannot skip bases. Becoming near world-class is akin to being on third base. But, to reach third base, you already need to be standing on second base.

> *"There seems to be some perverse human characteristic that likes to make easy things difficult."*
>
> *Warren Buffet*

The business was struggling and was getting out-sold and out-marketed even though it had superior products and reliability. The President realized that it had a weak sales team and poor sales and marketing presence. The solution agreed to was to immediately implement Salesforce.com, a CRM (Customer Relationship Management) program. With this program, the President felt that the sales team would be able to track customers and customer activities better, and sell and market better.

Alas, the project was a failure and abandoned within one year. In retrospect, it is obvious that the company was not able to implement the solution proposed. The company was barely out of the batter's box on sales and marketing. Full implementation of a productive sales and marketing effort with Salesforce.com is third base. To even begin working on the CRM solution, the company needed to be at second base. But, to get to second base, they first needed to ensure that top management had a commitment to customer service and sales. Then, they needed to get decent sales management in place to oversee and evaluate the sales team. Then, they needed to ensure that they had the right people on the sales team, who were properly trained on how to sell the products. Then, these salespeople needed to develop the discipline to diligently record their contacts in a simple database or Microsoft Outlook and to write sales reports. By this point, they may have finally been ready to implement Salesforce. com or another CRM program.

By shooting for a world-class solution, this change initiative was worse than "much ado about nothing", as it diverted attention and resources away from more critical needs and frustrated and exhausted the employees who worked on the initiative.

> *"There is a maxim; 80% strategy with 100% execution will win over 100% strategy with 80% execution."*
>
> **Eugene Lee**

Today, a few businesses have realized the importance of not always shooting for perfection. These businesses tend to look for the "80 / 100 solution" to problems. This is a solution that is not perfect but resolves 80% of the problem with the caveat that the solution is straightforward and simple enough that it can be 100% implemented by the people who are required to implement it.

Complexity Sells

The second reason for the relentless drive towards greater complexity in business is that complexity sells. Complexity is often the sizzle that sells the steak, especially with consultants. Having worked in consulting and been a part of internal teams that worked with consultants, I have witnessed far too often how consulting solutions are sold.

The consultants peddle a "solution" to a company's problem. For both the consulting firm and the business leader who hired them, this solution has to be perceived as being reasonably complex and difficult. Without sufficient complexity and "intellectual rigor", the consulting firm will not be perceived by the company to be adding any value. For the business leader, the solution needs to be complex to justify the expense of bringing in consultants to solve a problem that, in many instances, can be boiled down to one root cause: the management that brought in the consultants is under-performing in its job of leading the business.

But, if you strive to simplify this complexity in business you get tremendous push-back: push-back from the Consultant Salesperson that you are not taking advantage of all that their solution has to offer; push-back internally that you are not being ambitious enough. What is forgotten in this push towards a complex solution is the difficulty of the people on the front line that have to implement the solution and live with it on a daily basis. Better a simpler solution fully implemented than a complex, time-consuming one never completed.

I give two examples:

> When we were deciding on an Enterprise Software system (ERP) in the early 2000's, we did a beauty contest of the top three vendors. Our CEO asked each vendor to demonstrate the steps in the system to select ("pick") a product from inventory to be sold and then record the sale of that product. The highly paid consultants at the two largest vendors (both household names) could not complete the

demonstration; they did not themselves know how to do it. Their job was to sell and demonstrate all the sexiness of these complex programs to top managers to persuade them to buy the program. The details on the most fundamental task any ERP system can perform – enable a product to be sold and then to properly record that sale – was a mere afterthought.

A few years ago, four of my companies successfully rolled out Salesforce.com as a CRM solution. At that time, we were standing on second base and capable of rolling it out. In adapting Salesforce.com for our team, we chose to keep things as simple as we felt that we possibly could. So, we chose fewer than 20% of the features and fields available completely hiding the other 80%. The consultants and the team at Salesforce.com (both of whom did a great job in the rollout) remained convinced that we had dumbed-down the system too much. Nevertheless, in a post-mortem about the roll-out, the sales team's comments were nearly unanimous. The program was excellent and real progress, but the transition was difficult and prolonged because there were so many new features and fields.

American Culture

As commented on by many Europeans and written by Timothy Ferriss in his book, *The 4-Hour Workweek*, American culture tends to reward personal sacrifice instead of personal productivity or effectiveness. There is a real American trait that lauds those who achieve success through sheer hard work. Think of the start-up overwork ethic that entrepreneurs wear as badges of honor. Think of the "rites of passage" of medical interns and residents, first and second year lawyers, and investment bankers. Think of the point of pride of many business leaders to constantly be busy and check in at the office even while on vacation.

The overwhelming belief is that the harder that you work the more you will get done the better you will make your business. The question that is rarely asked is whether all this extra work is justified by improved business performance.

Bias for Action

Business leaders today are usually driven and love to work hard. With that comes a passion for getting things done or making it happen. As a result, business leaders have a real bias for action. If there is nothing to be done, many times they will find something to do and then do it.

> *"Most of what we call management today consists of making it difficult for people to get their work done."*
>
> **Peter Drucker**

Alas, a dirty little secret of business is that a business leader (above the level of first line P&L) running a good business should have time on his hands where he quite literally has little or nothing to do. The simple reason is that a business leader needs to let his people do their job and run their businesses.

One part of my Division consisted of four companies focused on the telecommunications infrastructure business. By 2004, I was fortunate to have a strong team of General Managers running these companies. It turns out that there is a curious seasonality in our little area of the telecommunications infrastructure business; year after year 40% of all sales occur and all work gets done in the months of November and December. As such, during that time, my General Managers were running "redline" to produce and ship product and complete projects and jobs as effectively as they could. Meanwhile, my role was "to let the stallions run." It was my job to support the team and run interference so that they could get done what needed to get done. Any new requirement, report, initiative from me would have distracted the team from serving the customer.

The first year or two that I did this felt awkward. I am supposed to work. I am too "important." I am too "valuable." I need to be

> a leader in charge doing stuff. Make it Happen!! Yet, the positive
> feedback and gratitude from the General Managers and the team was
> so strong, and the results were so compelling that I realized that not
> doing something can be as valuable as doing something.

What leaders with a bias for action may not realize is that any action that they take is multiplied ten to fifty times further down in the organization as everyone strives to satisfy the request or initiative. Time and (more importantly) attention span are finite so this extra work takes the focus away from other, likely more important aspects of the business. For the employee on the front line this bias for action often appears to be a daily deluge of change as they are being constantly required to learn something new or do something different. If you only take one idea away from reading this book, let it be about the value of keeping things simple and focusing on the few important issues.

To keep that focus, constantly ask yourself:

Is what I am doing right now moving the business closer to achieving its three goals?

Who Is My Target Audience?

My target audience is managers and business leaders with profit and loss responsibility who are leading businesses with annual revenue from $10M - $300M, primarily in the B2B (business–to–business) sector. These leaders are leading their team and leading other leaders. They are working on the business, not in the business. But, at the same time, they get into the "muck" of the business and stay abreast of what goes on in the trenches of their businesses.

As seen from my biography, I have the background and experience to relate to this target audience. Others are invited to read the book as well. Much of what I write may be relevant to leaders of larger businesses and business units, to leaders in the B2C (business–to–consumers) world, to leaders in government, and to leaders around the world. But, I cannot be sure. I just don't have sufficient experience in these areas. To avoid possibly shooting myself in the foot, I will stick to and focus on the areas that I do know.

SECTION II –
BUSINESS LEADERSHIP

Chapter 3 – The Goal of Business Leadership

"Everything rises and falls on leadership."

John Maxwell

- *What is the goal of business leadership?*
- *What is a Winning Business?*
- *The Fundamentals of a Winning Business*

What is the Goal of Business Leadership?

The goal of business leadership is simple – to build and improve a successful and winning business. Over the medium to long term, the success and failure of any business depends completely on the leadership of that business.

- If your business continues to succeed year after year, congratulations you have done well. Celebrate!!
- If your business is stuck in a rut, it is your job as a leader to get it out of the rut and back on track. You are not leading well enough.
- If your business continues to fail, is not growing, and is not making budgets, then you are failing as a leader.

The frustrating thing about business is that, in the short term, poor leaders can be phenomenally successful or just plain lucky and win big. In the short term, if they were smart, they sold out. Yes, some businesses may have it easier; they are in growing markets; they have a great niche. But, they or a predecessor did something right to get in that favorable competitive position.

At the same time, some business can fail for a while in the short-term. But, if they are led correctly, they will succeed in the medium and long term. The perfect example to that is GE's nuclear business. As their former CEO Jack Welch relates, they created a successful business in an absolutely no-growth industry. The fundamental assumption in their business model was that their core US customers would never again build another nuclear plant. Yet, through excellent leadership, they still were successful.

So I repeat, over the medium to long term, whether your business wins or loses depends completely on your leadership.

But, what is winning?

What is a Winning Business?

In defining a winning business, I have combined my fundamentals with ideas from Ken Blanchard's *Leading at a Higher Level*. A winning business is a business that becomes and remains:

Investment of Choice

The business is ethical and respectful of all stakeholders. The business makes a strong return on investment, both in profit and cash flow. The business continues to grow in sales, profits and cash flow.

Employer of Choice

There are "A" players throughout the business. The business culture is positive, accountable, and reinforcing. "A" players want to work in the business.

<u>Supplier of Choice</u>

The business supplies a product or provides a service that is valued in the marketplace. Customers think of the business first when they are making their buying decision. The reputation and brand of the business has value that customers are willing to pay a premium for and that differentiates the business from others in the market.

A business focused on each and all of these goals will win in the short, medium and long term.

Do not under-estimate the challenge of building a winning business. In sports, winning one championship in one season can define a successful career. In business, you have to win over and over. In every year, every month, every interaction, you have to prove once again that your business deserves to be considered an investment, an employer and a supplier of choice.

The Fundamentals of a Winning Business

The only way to ensure that your business will continue to achieve these momentary, monthly and yearly victories is to develop a culture in your business based on the fundamentals:

- Fundamentals that are rock-solid, easily understood, easily communicated, and easily kept front of mind.
- Fundamentals that dovetail with the definition of a winning business.
- Fundamentals that act as the filter through which all decisions and activities of the company pass.

For me, these three fundamentals are:

I. <u>Do the Right Thing</u>
   a. Ethics, Integrity, and Honesty
   b. Determine Your Values and Goals for the Business
   c. Align the Organization to Live the Values and Focus on the Goals

2. <u>Winning Teamwork</u>
    a. Communication
    b. Accountability
    c. Motivate and Engage the Team
    d. Recognition
    e. Continuous Learning

3. <u>Customer Service</u>
    a. Value Your Customers
    b. Satisfy Your Current Customers' Needs
    c. Grow Outward from Your Customers Base

In most of the rest of the book, we will discuss these three fundamentals in detail. But, first we must discuss some business leadership fundamentals and the roles of the leader and the leadership team.

CHAPTER 4 –
THE FUNDAMENTALS OF
BUSINESS LEADERSHIP

"There is a real difference between managing and leading. Managing winds up being the allocation of resources against tasks. Leadership focuses on people. My definition of a leader is someone who helps people succeed."

Carol Bartz (CEO, Autodesk and Yahoo)

Many people, far smarter and far more talented than I, have been grappling with the question of business management and business leadership. To be honest, I do not understand much of what is written. So, I will not try to address and solve that problem here. Instead, I want to discuss some of the basics of business leadership that once mastered will move your business forward and help you be more successful in achieving the three fundamentals of a winning business.

1. The management toolkit

2. Leadership 101

3. The importance of example

4. Working through your leadership team

CHAPTER 5 – THE MANAGEMENT TOOLKIT

> "The fortune is in the follow-up."

Anonymous

- *Set a Goal*
- *Follow Up*
- *Provide Support and Feedback*

In this chapter, I discuss the basic management behaviors of setting goals, following-up, and then providing support and feedback. The proper and constant use of these management behaviors goes a long way towards making someone an effective leader.

Set a Goal

In setting specific goals for your team, be clear, precise and detailed.

- Who?
- What?
- When?
- How Important?

From my experience, leaders clearly explain the Who? and the What? But, they may neglect to mention when the goal needs to be achieved (When?). And, they often forget to explain how critical the goal is (How Important?). It is crucial to communicate the relative importance of a goal and the tasks to achieve that goal. This allows the team to know which goals are more important and settle any conflicting priorities.

Further, in setting any goal, the leader needs to be certain that...

- The team knows how to get the task done.
- The team has all the resources to get the job done.
- The team accepts the goal and commits to getting it done in the time frame specified.

Follow-Up

Once a goal is set and agreed to, the most important leadership skill is following up. This is the skill that most of us often do intermittently. But, it is essential to follow-up to ensure that the progress towards the goal is on track. At the very least, the leader needs to follow up before the due date to ensure that the project will get done by that due date and the goal achieved.

> *"You should never aspire to be a manager or an executive if you don't do follow-up. You won't be happy, and you won't do a good job, because that's what leaders do most of the time."*
>
> *Martin Zwilling*

Follow-Up is so crucial for several reasons:

- In general, people are over-confident and believe that, even when behind, they will catch up. In reality, once tasks or projects are behind they generally stay behind.
- The vast majority of people do not like to tell unsolicited bad news to the boss. So, even though there might be a problem, they would not tell the leader about it until he asks.

- Lack of follow-up from the leader is often interpreted by the team as a shift in priorities from the leader. Since so many leaders forget goals or assignments that they have made, the team quite rightly concludes that the leader has forgotten about the project. So they forget about the project as well. Lou Gerstner, former CEO of IBM, once said that "people respect what you inspect not what you expect." So, inspect and follow up to ensure that they respect the goal that you set out.

As a last point on follow-up, avoid playing the fun game of "Gotcha." Gotcha occurs when leaders give a long term assignment and then never mention it again. On the due date, they get furious and rant and rave because the assignment was not completed. By playing this game, not only is the goal not achieved but the leader's credibility is damaged.

Provide Support and Feedback

In helping the team achieve the goal as originally set out, the leader needs to provide support and feedback. The support comes in several forms:

- **Help the team get the time and resources** to complete the task. Often, this needs to include shifting priorities and reducing time commitments on other goals to ensure that the goal in question can be completed.
- **Coach the team** to develop their skills and help them think through issues. This usually involves questioning and asking the team how they would work through a problem.
- **Ensure success**. When the goal is not getting completed, the leader needs to lend a hand to help determine why things are not getting done and to help determine what needs to change to get things done.

- **Problem solving assistance.** When needed, the leader lends his expertise to directly help resolve problems which have come up.

In addition, providing feedback on the work done is absolutely vital. It can be done in many ways.

- Positive feedback or recognition
- Negative feedback or suggestions for improvement
- Formal and informal post-mortems of the work done to record lessons learned for later work

Chapter 6 –
Leadership 101

"When the best leader's work is done, the
people say: 'we did it ourselves.'"

Lao-Tzu

- *Quick Quiz on leadership*
- *Situational leadership*
- *Mantra*

Quick Quiz on Leadership

True or False:
You should manage and lead by the "Golden Rule." That is,
you should manage and lead others as you would want to be
managed or led?
The answer to this question is **False**.

Yes, you should always manage and lead others with respect and
dignity. But, the way that you manage others should be based on
how they need to be managed or led to allow the business to execute
on its goals.

As a leader, you need to use "Situational Leadership" with your
team.

Situational Leadership

The concept of Situational Leadership was conceived by Ken Blanchard in his book: *Leadership and the One Minute Manager.* Having used Situational Leadership for seven years in managing my General Managers and direct reports, I present a slightly modified version of the concept which has served me well.

In general, there are six leadership styles that you use depending on the individual that you are leading:

1. Dictative
    a. The leader just dictates to the team what needs to be done. There are no questions, no comments, and no suggestions. It is top down.
    b. "Do what I say or else."

2. Directive
    a. The leader directs the team very closely using the management tool-kit as discussed above on nearly all important matters.
    b. Key words would be: structure, organize, teach and train, supervise, continuous follow-up.

> *In leading others, you need to use "different strokes for different folks."*
>
> **Ken Blanchard**

3. Coaching
    a. The leader still closely monitors the team's activities with precise goal-setting, but gives the team latitude in how they accomplish the goals.
    b. The employees' ideas are considered. When there are problems or issues that need the leader's insight or approval, the employees are encouraged to come with both a description of the problem and the pros and cons of their proposed solution.

4. <u>Supportive</u>
    a. The leader provides broader goals letting the team provide the more specific goals. The team has broader latitude to decide how to accomplish the broader goals.
    b. Employees are still asked to come to the leader with both the problem and the solution. But, the nature of the problem is generally more complex than in the Coaching style.

5. <u>Delegative</u>
    a. The leader turns over the responsibility of much of the decision making to the subordinate or team.
    b. The leader remains engaged with what is going on and still follows up on a regular basis, but generally does not get involved in the details of issues unless asked to by the team.
    c. The leader is a sounding board for the subordinate and team on the most vexing problems and issues, and will make big decisions if that is what the subordinates want.

6. <u>Abandon</u>
    a. The leader lets the subordinate or team run the business as they see fit.
    b. The leader will still monitor the results of the business, but plays no active role in moving the business forward. There is little, if any, follow-up.
    c. In this case, although the subordinate or team nominally reports to the leader, they are not taking any advantage of the strengths and insight of the leader.
    d. This is a very hands-off leadership style

The first and last style of leadership, dictative and abandon, should be avoided. In the dictative, your subordinates and team add no value; you are deciding what needs to be done and then ordering that it be done. In the abandon style, you, as the leader, are offering no value; you have abdicated your role as a leader letting your subordinates and team do what they want.

Many of you may be familiar with an even worse form of leadership: "pigeon leadership." Pigeon leadership takes the worst of both the dictative and abandon style of leadership and combines them. With pigeon leadership, the leader ignores the business completely until something goes wrong, he then swoops in to visit the business unit, sh*ts on everyone screaming and yelling and dictating what needs to be done to correct the problems. With the dictative part over, he then flies away, satisfied that he has shown the team what leadership is all about and proceeds to abandon the business unit once again until the next problem occurs. All bark and no bite.

To help his team become as successful as possible, a leader will often need to use "different strokes for the same folk."

All of the other leadership styles are needed. The choice of leadership style to use depends on the broad tasks and the individual employees' preferences and abilities.

- Preferences: What does the employee like to do and what does he not like to do? In general, all of us inevitably gravitate to do what we like to do first and generally do this better.
- Abilities: In what areas, does the employee have the skills and knowledge to succeed? In what areas, are the skills and knowledge of the employee still being developed?

Let's consider a simplified example of leading General Managers with full P&L responsibility for both operations and sales and marketing. My experience is that no individual is equally adept and equally passionate at both operations and sales. As such, the leadership style needs to reflect the relative passion (preference) and relative capabilities (ability) of the General Manager.

- Consider a reasonably new General Manager who came up through operations. On operational issues, you might use the coaching style and then evolve to the supportive style as he becomes familiar with his new role in overseeing operational issues. For sales, you would likely be quite directive as this is a new area where he has little experience and may or may not have the passion.

- Consider an experienced General Manager who came up through and has a passion for and a history of success with sales. You might be delegative on the sales side. Yet, even though he is an experienced General Manager, you might remain either directive or coaching on operational issues.

Three points to consider:

1. When using the coaching and supportive style, you will likely push and nudge the individual to do what you want him to do. But, resist reverting to the directive style to "just get this one thing done." Even if done rarely, this becomes the expectation of the individual and undercuts the person's sense of ownership and accountability. One of the most difficult challenges in being a leader is to see something that is not exactly as you want it to be and to say nothing to avoid usurping the empowered person's authority.

2. Communicate the approach you will be taking ahead of time so that a directive style in one area is not perceived as an overall directive style and thus considered either micro-managing or meddling. Once written down, nearly all managers and employees will understand the purpose and the reasons behind the different approaches.

3. Encourage two-way communication to avoid conflicts about how you are leading someone. If the employee feels that he has evolved and should now be managed with the delegative style, then he needs to communicate that. If you disagree, you need to communicate why you will continue using the coaching or supportive style.

The value in the situational leadership approach is two-fold. First, you realize the differences of each subordinate and, accordingly, manage them differently. Second, it allows you as the manager to dedicate the time and effort to assist each subordinate in the most important areas he needs to be assisted in.

Mantra

With more experienced employees or leaders, there will be occasions where they know what needs to be done in a certain part of the business and how to do it. But, they just do not do it. Oftentimes, it is because that part of the business is one that they are less comfortable with and one that they may not enjoy doing. Consider the example of an operationally-focused General Manager that may not spend enough time improving sales and marketing.

Because of the experience and maturity of the leader, the directive style may have limited use. It is not that they do not know how to do it; they just need to be convinced that this part of the business needs more of their time and attention. Suggestions and statements about "first things first" or "our job is not to do what we want to do but instead do what we need to do" may have limited usefulness. To ensure that this part of the business gets sufficient attention, you may want to consider making it a "mantra."

The concept of mantra first came into the public eye in the US in the 1970's with the introduction of transcendental meditation. In it, you focus on one word, a mantra, which you repeat over and over again to help you achieve higher levels of relaxation and consciousness. Achieving higher levels of consciousness is slightly outside the scope of this book. Nevertheless, the concept of repeat repeat repeating something almost to ad nauseum is an important management tool that complements situational leadership.

In our example, assume that the operations are doing well. But, the sales and marketing is not progressing. In using the Mantra, you would back off from focusing on the operations and other matters and begin to focus laser-like on increasing the General Manager's time and attention to sales and market and thus hopefully improve the results. As such, sales and marketing becomes your Mantra for this General Manager.

- Set performance goals disproportionally directed towards sales and marketing and follow up with interim performance reviews on sales and marketing
- Begin and end meetings with the topic of sales and marketing
- Ask similar key questions repeatedly:
  o How are you getting involved with sales and marketing?
  o Have you visited with customers recently?
  o Has customer satisfaction improved?
  o What new customers and market are we penetrating?
- Offer assistance and be a sounding board on sales and marketing
- Set up joint meetings with customers and this General Manager

In using a Mantra, you are not being directive as the person still will be deciding what must be done to achieve the goals. But, you are being insistent that attention be paid to that one area. To use effectively, focus on only one part of the business and reduce somewhat the focus on other parts. And it is important to use for a significant amount of time, six months to a year, both to ensure that the problem is truly resolved and to avoid having it appear to be a case of management "theme of the month."

Yes, when done poorly it can be interpreted as micro-management and be infuriating for the subordinate. But, your job as a leader is to make your people better and the business better. Through the correct use of a Mantra, you will get the attention and focus your people need to do exactly that.

CHAPTER 7 – THE IMPORTANCE OF YOUR EXAMPLE

"Example is not the main thing in influencing others.
It is the only thing. Example is leadership."

Albert Schweitzer

- *Role of the business leader*
- *Lead by example*
- *Be Responsive*

Role of the Business Leader

In the last few chapters, we have been talking about leadership behaviors. I want to take a step back and think about the role of the business leader. I am not talking about a good business leader as a sole proprietor. I am discussing an effective business leader that must work through people to realize success.

What is the role of the business leader? A business leader must use everything at his disposal:

- His insight and intellect
- His personality
- His attention

- His communication skills
- His example

... to make his people successful, which in turn makes his business successful, which in turn makes the business leader successful.

This is a crucial tenet of my view of business leadership. You can call it servant leadership. You can call it anything you want. But, fundamentally the job of the business leader is to build success through his people. But, his people will only thrive if they are in a winning organizational culture based on the three fundamentals of doing the right thing, winning teamwork, and customer service.

Lead by Example

The organizational culture always reflects the leader. Thus, the successful leader has to be (and be seen as) the **example** for the entire organization. He needs to live, breathe, sweat and bleed these three fundamentals. Only then, will the organization live, breathe, sweat and bleed these fundamentals as well.

Unfortunately, leading by example (and making it visible) is one thing at which many leaders fail!

Quick Quiz on Leading by Example

1. Can you recall three examples where your ethics visibly showed through to the team?

2. Do you return everyone's phone calls immediately and respond to all E-Mails promptly? Do you start and finish meetings promptly?

3. Right now, does your front-line management have fewer than five goals?

4. In the last month, have you communicated your values to your team other than in a general E-Mail or announcement?

5. As a leader, do you take full accountability for the failures, but share the praise for the successes?

6. Have you ensured that all of your senior direct reports are held accountable for their performance?

7. In the last week, have you found at least ten people doing something right and recognized and thanked them for their work?

8. In the last month, have you coached, trained and taught at least one small group in your business?

9. Are you easy to reach and interact with? That is, are you personally easy to do business with?

10. In the last two weeks, have you been involved in resolving a customer service issue?

11. In the last two weeks, have you been involved in thanking a good customer for their business?

O.K. Does anyone have all "Yes" answers? I do not think so. Side note: I must admit that, as a leader, I do not have all "Yes" answers either.

Now, switch roles and think of yourself as an employee or manager working for a leader that can answer "Yes" to all the questions:
- Would this be a good leader to work for?
- Would you know what the leader stands for?
- Would you think that, over time, this business will be successful with this leader?

The behaviors in the quiz are all behaviors that most leaders would agree are instrumental in building a successful business. They are likely already on the To-Do lists of many leaders today. Unfortunately, for many leaders, they remain the ideal rather than the reality. They intend to do them, but just do not get them done.

> *We judge ourselves by our intentions; others judge us by our actions. Wrong actions done by a leader with the absolute best of intentions still remain detrimental to the business and the leader.*

Yet, each time that the leader falls short on one of these issues, he loses some of his authority and some of his influence. The example of the leader in all that he does, big and small, is of paramount importance. Whether the leader likes it or not, he is always on stage and always leading by his example.

To drill home this point, I discuss one of the most common leadership failings in business today – the inability of leaders and businesspeople to be responsive and return phone calls and promptly reply to E-Mails. Some people would consider this example to be trivial. I disagree. Business is all about the other person whether it be the customer or the employee. A lack of responsiveness by a leader easily leads to a cultural norm that what we are doing is more important than what they – the customer, the employee, the stakeholder – need from us.

Be Responsive

<u>Return Phone Calls</u>

"Your call is very important to me. Please leave your message, and I will get back to you as soon as I can. Thank you."

Welcome to the biggest lie in business!!

Every day, leaders are not returning phone calls or replying to E-Mails. This guarantees sub-standard performance from you as a leader and your organization for several reasons:

- Every day, it sets and reinforces a perfect example of **lack of accountability**. You, your people, and your company are not doing what was said.
- **It kills time**. Urgent issues are not promptly addressed. Due to all the delays, tasks that can be done reasonably quickly drag out or are not done at all.
- **It is rude** and you are not easy to do business with.
- **It increases inefficiency**. People will leave multiple messages, just to get ahead in the queue. E-Mails fly about that are read by fewer than half the people in the group. Supervisors waste time holding meetings to repeat things already written in E-Mails in order to be sure that the message is communicated because people are not reading their E-Mails.

Guess what? Immediately returning your phone calls and replying to E-Mails will make your life much easier and simpler. How do I know? I know, because I have being doing this for 17 years.

In the early 1990's, I read an article about the Hollywood agent business and Michael Ovitz's CAA. In the article, it was mentioned that all CAA agents were required to return all their clients' calls by the end of the day or they could be fired. Working in a bureaucratic organization at the time, this sentiment resonated.

As such, I came up with a simple statement which I then shared with everyone (colleagues, employees, customers, suppliers):

> I will return your phone call within 24 hours (by the same time the next business day) or I will pay you $100.

This was a simple statement that is actually quite simple to do (most of the time). In the last 17 years, I have written a $100 check once, but the person involved refused to cash it. After receiving the check from me, he found out that while I had not gotten back to him directly within 24 hours, I had left 3 messages with his assistant who had failed to relay these messages on to him. I really wanted him to cash the check, because it was my responsibility to get back to him, and I did not. I also wanted him to cash the check because for $100 it would make the story stick and reverberate with everyone in my division.

As the President of a $200M division, the reaction from most people the first time I return their call promptly is usually shock.

> Oh my gosh, I did not expect your call.

> I cannot believe that you actually called me back.

> Thank you very much.

For customers, it is truly win-win, they are so appreciative to have somebody actually return their phone call, actually speak to them, and actually address their concerns that you and your company's rating with them as a supplier sky-rockets.

Yes, it can be a pain. On business in Europe, being up in your room at 1:00 a.m. responding to routine calls. But, that does not happen as much as you would think. And, even if you get voice mail when returning the call, you can leave a powerful message to your customer, supplier or employee that they matter.

> Sarah, I know it is 6:00 pm where you are but I was hoping that I could get you. I am returning your phone call from earlier today. I am on business over here in Ireland. But, I will be up for another hour so if you get this give me a call back and we can talk.

But, I hear you saying: "I get so many calls that I cannot possibly return all of them."

That will be a challenge at the beginning until you set out the rules of the road in your company, with suppliers, and with salespeople. Customers can also be cautiously and carefully trained, but that is less important since they are your customers and you want to be responsive to them under all circumstances.

Some rules to reduce the call volume and make you and your team more effective:

- *Require People to Leave a Real Message About What They Want or Need.*

    Leaving a substantive message allows you to think about the response and get to the point when you call them back. No more: "Hi, this is David. Can you give me a call back?"Better: "Hi, this is David. We just had another large order from a solar company. As such, I am beginning a marketing campaign focused on alternative energy (solar and wind). I want to get your marketing insight on our approach. Please call me back to discuss."

- *Batch (or Aggregate) Phone Calls and Communication*

    Unless urgent, require your people to call you only once about 3 items instead of three times about one item each time. As the leader, this applies to you. Do not constantly be calling and disturbing your team. Aggregate your own communication, calling them when you have multiple things to discuss.

- *Get to the Point in All Conversations and in Call-backs.*

    If you get voice mail when you call back, then leave a substantive message as this can often resolve the issue in question without further phone calls.

- *Require Salespeople That Call You to Do Some Work and Follow Up in Order to Earn the Time to Talk to You*

    My preferred method is to call back a salesperson and tell him that I would like a one-page summary of what they are offering and why I should be interested sent to my E-Mail within one day. If they do that, I would then talk to them.

If not, I will not be talking to them. My experience is that 95% of all salespeople will not complete this simple task. As such, the other 5% would be the only ones worth talking to. To the point - yes. Polite – maybe. Effective – yes.

Reply to E-Mails Promptly

The goal at the end of every business day should be to have **no** E-Mails in the In-Box. That is the goal. You should always have fewer than 10.

How?

- *Be Organized. Be Ruthless.*

   Scan your E-Mails for the ones that are most important first. Read them once. Act on them. Delete the E-Mail. Repeat with the E-Mails that are most urgent. If you cannot immediately act on a particular E-Mail, set up a To-Do task and schedule a time that you are going to finish this task. Save any content that you need on your computer. Then delete the E-Mail. Don't think about the task until it is the scheduled time. Fly through any E-Mails where you are cc: or any E-Mails that are just "For your information". Skim through. Get the gist. Delete. Move on.

- *Require That You or Your Team Resolve the Issues on the E-Mail or Suggest Solutions*

   As mentioned before, I require that the direct reports come with their solution to any problem that they want my input on. Not only does this improve their strategic thinking and give them greater ownership of the solution, it also led to quicker resolution of the issues. By resolving and suggesting solutions, you avoid the endless and useless streams of E-Mail, all of which really only say:

Yes, I read this E-Mail. I am passing my empty thoughts on to all of you for no reason other than to ensure that you know that I read the E-Mail and that my butt is covered.

With these tactics, 95% of your E-Mails can be responded to and dispatched very quickly.   To paraphrase General George Patton:

> A good response, violently executed now, is better than a perfect response next week.

I know. I know. I will now climb down from my soapbox after making three final comments about returning phone calls and replying to E-Mails.

First, as a leader you never want to be the cog in the wheel, the rate determining step holding up the flow of work. In business, time is the most over-looked element.   Your slow response can literally have 10 expensive people twiddling their thumbs for a day waiting for you to get back to them: ten people for one day at (say) $80,000 a year; that equals $3,200. $3,200 pissed away. Another customer potentially pissed off.

Second, if you really try, but are unable to return phone calls and answer back E-Mails promptly without spending all day and night engrossed in your I-Phone or Droid, then you need to think about why this is so.

- You may be patently un-organized.
- You may be in too many meetings.
- You may have too much going on and thus are not prioritizing on the few critical issues.
- You may not delegate well enough.
- You may micro-manage and be too involved in what your team is doing.
- Or, as in the case of a failing colleague of mine who I once observed had 2,452 E-Mails in his In-Box, you may be all these things.

Third, I am not quite alone in my view of phone calls and E-Mails. In his book, *Ahead of the Curve: Two Years at Harvard Business School*, Philip Delves Brought on relates some advice he got from Dan Gilbert, CEO of Quicken Loans.

> Return calls and E-Mails in a timely way. That would put you 99.9%
> ahead of your competitors. People are shocked; people are in awe
> when you do this. They can't believe it. And we can't believe that
> people can't believe it because we think everybody should do it.

Likewise, in a 2010 article in *Fortune,* Wal-Mart CEO Mike Duke states:

> I keep up with E-Mails. I don't like carry overs. At the end of the
> day, I don't want there to be any phone messages that haven't been
> returned or E-Mails that aren't addressed.

Of course, returning phone calls and responding to E-Mails will not, in and of themselves, make you an effective business leader. But, not returning phone calls and responding to E-Mails will all but guarantee that you are (at best) a sub-optimal business leader.

Chapter 8 – Work Through Your Leadership Team

"Trust but Verify"

President Ronald Reagan

- *Quick quiz about leadership*
- *Aligning the leadership team*
- *Know how your managers are managing*

Congratulations!! You have read through the previous chapters and realize that you use the basic management tools adeptly, that you use situational leadership (even if you did not call it that), and that you generally do what you say and lead by your nearly immaculate example. Great Job!!

Before we move on, let's take a quick quiz:

Quick Quiz about Leadership

I. Grade your own personal job performance:
- A = 4
- B = 3
- C = 2

- $D = 1$
- $F = 0$

2. Average the grade of your direct reports in their job performance:
   a. $A = 4$
   b. $B = 3$
   c. $C = 2$
   d. $D = 1$
   e. $F = 0$

3. Subtract the number in 2 from the number in 1

4. Write the number in 3 on a piece of paper

I have given this quiz dozens of time to managers at all levels during leadership training classes. The answers have varied from -2 all the way to 4.

What is your answer?

Except where the leader is new to his role, the "correct" answer is 0. If your direct reports are doing "C" work, then you are only a "C" leader as $2 - 2 = 0$.

Extend this concept down to the trenches. If you believe that your company and your sales, operations and other employees are only doing "C" or "D" jobs, then, face reality, you are only doing a "C" or "D" job as a leader.[2]

In short, you personally can be incredibly dynamic and brilliant, but you are only as good as your team. The fundamental postulate of business leadership remains the same:

---

2   Having once had a 35 minute "discussion" after a training session with one leader who insisted that his answer of 4 was correct (he was an "A" and his team was an "F"), I have also used this test to determine the appropriateness of certain individuals for a leadership position.

> For a leader to be successful in the medium to long term, his employees have to be successful, his management team has to be successful, and his business has to be successful.

Some of you may disagree. You may feel that business leaders are great people who move mountains and make all the difference.

- The turn-around expert
- The great entrepreneur
- The "genius with a thousand helpers"

These "superstar" leaders can be tremendously successful at improving a business or building a business to a certain level. But, as the business gets larger and more complex, the daily influence and contribution of any leader trails off and needs to be picked up by the team.

> On two of the turnarounds that my team accomplished, we came in and managed directively. Quite frankly, we acted at times like the "geniuses." With both of these businesses relatively small (average of $15M in revenue), bleeding money and with such low hanging fruit, I still feel that this was the right course of action.

> These times were truly exhilarating. Working eighteen hour days, we could see day to day the improvements that we were making as the businesses stabilized and became profitable. The challenge came once the ship was righted and the low hanging fruit was all plucked. Then, it became necessary to change leadership styles and work with and build the team to ensure long term success. Especially, in the first acquisition, we struggled for quite a while to make this transition.

> *"The hardest part of a business transformation is changing the culture — the mindset and instincts of the people in the company."*
>
> **Lou Gerstner**

In most dramatic turn-arounds it is this transition from lone hero leader to a team-focused leader that is the most difficult part. But, for long term success it has to be done.

Later, we will discuss the importance of leading, developing, and aligning your employees into a Winning Team. For now, I would like to focus on you and your leadership team. Does your leadership team share your values and support your business goals? Are you and your leadership team in alignment?

Align Your Leadership Team

In any business larger than $20M in sales, it is unlikely that you are managing and leading all your employees directly. There is at least one layer of managers between you and the employees on the front line: the engineers, production workers, sales and marketing people, who are actually getting the work done.

> *"High performance teams and organizations are built of people, plans, and practices aligned around a shared purpose."*
>
> *George Bradt*

So, how do you know that the message that you are sending out is being communicated in the way that you want it to be communicated to your entire team?

This is one of the more challenging and least discussed areas of business. How do you get alignment in values and goals across an organization?

To be as effective as possible, an organization has to have this alignment. It is this alignment and this focus that allows an organization to win by:

- Sharing the same concept of ethics and integrity.
- All aiming to achieve the same business goals.
- Building a team that is greater than the sum of its parts.
- Interacting with one voice and one brand message to the customer.

I give two examples that highlight the organizational misalignment that is all too common in business.

The first example concerns a Divisional President colleague who had a struggling business.

> This colleague went down to the facility and spent a day asking just two questions to employees:
>
> 1.   What are the three critical issues with this business?
>
> 2.   What are your three biggest priorities?
>
> The questions were asked of the General Manager, individuals in every layer of management and individuals on the front line in all departments (sales, production, engineering, accounting, etc.). There was no agreement or alignment anywhere. As an example, in production, the General Manager, the plant manager, the production leadmen, and the production workers had no commonality to their answers. The three biggest priorities of the workers were not the biggest priorities of leadmen, which were not the biggest priorities of the plant manager, which were not the biggest production priorities of the General Manager. Is it any wonder that the business was losing money?

Second, in his book, *The 8th Habit*, Stephen Covey discusses the results of a survey that measured the level of alignment of employees in businesses to the business goals.

> If, say, a soccer team had these same scores,
>
> • Only 4 of the 11 players on the field would know which goal is theirs.
> • Only 2 of the 11 players would care.
> • Only 2 of the 11 would know what position they play and know exactly what they are supposed to do.
> • And all but 2 players would, in some way, be competing against their own team members rather than the opponent.

Wow!!

Quick Quiz: In both examples, who is responsible for this atrocious lack of alignment and the resulting dysfunction?

Answer: the business leader

So, how can you really know how your key managers are managing and whether they are in alignment with your values and goals?

Know How Your Managers are Managing

With a business larger than $20M, you have also delegated a large part of the running of the business to your key leadership team, some of whom may not be located in the same office, state or even country as you are. Most likely, you have a profit and loss statement and other accounting measures to determine whether the members of your leadership team are making their numbers. But, do you really know how these key managers are managing?

- Does your leadership team understand and share your values and goals?
- Does your leadership team interact with their subordinates in the outstanding, responsive, and enlightened way that you interact with them?
- Does your leadership team lead by their example?
- How do you know?
- How can you be sure?

A True Story

> A number of years ago, I took a 360 degree evaluation along with a group of other "high potentials." For those that may not know, a 360 degree evaluation combines a self-evaluation with the results of a survey and interviews with your supervisors, peers, and direct reports to give a complete picture of how you are as a leader. In any event, we received our 360 feedback at a leadership training seminar that

we all attended. As we were walking out of the meeting, a colleague pulled me aside to ask a sincere question about his results.

> In my 360, my supervisors and I both rated myself very highly. But my direct reports gave me very low marks. How can my supervisors and I be so right and my direct reports be so wrong? Since I am obviously doing well in my supervisor's eyes, why should I change my behavior based on the results of this 360?

This colleague is an example of every leader's fear about their key leadership team. Leaders fear that they have an executive who makes the numbers and looks good in the upward direction while destroying the culture and values that the leader is trying to embed in the organization. Kiss up, but kick down.

So, how can you get to the truth about your key executives, not only in terms of their results, but in terms of their example to their employees, their values and their goals?

As President Reagan said: "trust but verify."

There are three things that all leaders should be doing in managing their leadership team:

1. Ensure that your message is heard throughout the organization

2. Develop relationships with stakeholders down, across and outside the organization

3. Look the gift horse in the mouth

Ensure That Your Message is Heard Throughout the Organization

As the business leader, you define the values and goals of your company. And you need to ensure that everyone has heard and understood these values and goals, not only your direct reports, but also their direct reports and all stakeholders. If not, employees many levels down in the organization may just accept the toxic values of a poor supervisor as being your values as a leader and the values of the company.

But, defining values and setting business goals does no good unless these messages are heard. To ensure that your values and goals are heard you need to communicate, preach, discuss, teach. Jack Welch, the former CEO of GE, writes:

> There were times I talked about the company's direction so much that I was completely sick of hearing it myself.

While posters, signs and slogans may be nice and have their place, the message is best heard in person, face to face.

- *Manage by Walking Around (MBWA)*

     Get out of your office and engage with and ask questions to employees throughout the office, in the field, and on the factory floor. Preach the message. Share stories with the employees that embody the values and clarify the goals.

- *Teach Classes to Employees at All Levels of the Organization or Hold Skip-Level "Lunch and Learns"*

     By teaching and meeting directly with the team you can reinforce and explain the values and goals in more detail. This also gives the leader an opportunity to get to know individuals and to be known.

- *Repeat*

     Consider the "Power of Ten." This maxim of communication advises that a new concept or idea may need to be communicated as many as ten times before being internalized by the listeners. This repetition helps convince the team that the message is important to you and that you mean what you say.

<u>Develop Relationships with Stakeholders Down, Across and Outside the Organization</u>

You need to develop relationships with individuals one, two, three, four or more levels down in your organization. There need to be individuals many levels down in the organization that you can ask how things are going and get a reasonably honest answer. Likewise, you need to develop relationships with key suppliers and some key customers that will honestly tell you how your company is delivering on its promise.

Especially with individuals lower in the organization, you need to be careful that they are not perceived as spies. It is important not to undercut the authority of their supervisors, especially if you hear of a problem. And it is important that they do not take what you say out of context and run to their supervisors saying the equivalent of: "we can't do it this way. I just spoke with the President and in our discussion, he said that he disagreed and…"

There is a fine line between getting the truth from stakeholders and over-stepping your bounds, usurping the authority of their supervisors and micro-managing. But, it is a line that must be approached.

Some good questions to ask the employees in your organization:
- What is your biggest challenge today?
- Tell me what the values and goals of the company are? (This is a good question to measure alignment and confirm whether your message has been heard).
- What are your three biggest priorities? (Another alignment question)
- What can we as management do to help you do your job better?

After asking the questions, listen closely to the answers and don't offer to solve their problem (that is their supervisor's job). But, by listening you will get a clear picture of how things are going in that business unit.

Look the Gift Horse in the Mouth

The test in managing managers is not the manager who does not deliver on their numbers. We should all be able to deal with that. The challenge is with the manager who delivers on his numbers, but is toxic to the culture of the company.

Look these gift horses in the mouth. Trust and verify their behaviors and values with their subordinates and other stakeholders (as above). And importantly, listen and observe them in action.

- *Listen and Observe How They Get Their Job Done*
    Do they work in accordance with your values and goals? What do they say they spend their time on? What are the problems that they continue to have?
- *Listen to the Stories They Tell About Their Business and Their Team*
    Who is the hero in the story? The manager or the team? Do the stories show empathy to team members?
- *Observe Their Behavior With Others in the Office*
    In general, do they seem to be good guys or jerks? Are they friendly? Do they greet people by name? Do they know people's names?

If you still cannot get a comfortable feel about a manager and his values and style, then I would recommend doing a 360 degree evaluation for him. It is not a perfect tool; some stakeholders (especially subordinates) may not believe that the answers will remain confidential. But, it will give a fuller picture of the leader. There are 360's that can be taken on-line and ones that are taken with an outside firm. It does not need to be expensive; but can be quite useful.

In summary, the true strength and power in any successful organization comes from having all parts of the organization rowing in the same direction and in sync. This must start with the leadership team being in alignment with the values and goals of the leader. This does not mean that you want to create an organization of clones; you want and will almost certainly have leaders and managers with different styles and different personalities. Nevertheless, these key leaders must share and be aligned with the core values and support the direction and goals that you as the leader have chosen for the organization.

SECTION III – DO THE RIGHT THING

Chapter 9 – Do the Right Thing

"Do the right thing. It will gratify some
people and astonish the rest."

Mark Twain

The goal of "Do the Right Thing" is to create a business that is effective and that you can be proud of each and every day.

Three characteristics of doing the right thing are:

1. **Ethics, Integrity, and Honesty**
   Everything that we do should pass the newspaper front page test:

   > Would your actions today embarrass you tomorrow if they
   > appeared on the front page of your hometown newspaper?

   Be honest with yourself and everyone else. Seek out the "true" truth and foster candor within the organization

2. **Determine Your Values and Business Goals**
   Do the right thing for the business. Define core values. Create business goals to tackle the few critical issues and

opportunities for the business. Make the tough decisions to ensure the success and profitability of the business in both the short and the long term. If the business does not succeed, none of us do.

3.   **Align the Organization to Your Values and Goals**
Ensure everyone is in alignment to live the values and focus on and execute the goals. Consider the contributions of the team; focusing on what is achieved. Not, how busy they are. Prioritize on the constraint in the business – that which is important, not on what is most urgent. In prioritizing, consciously decide what not to do.

Chapter 10 – Ethics and Integrity

"We do not act rightly because we have virtue or excellence.
But, rather we have those because we have acted rightly."

Aristotle

- *Set the example of ethics and integrity*
- *Regularly talk about ethics*
- *Chase down ethical violations and air the dirty laundry*

The times are tough. The pressure on you and all your employees is intense. You have employees that cannot make the mortgage payments on their over-priced houses. You have managers that cannot make their numbers. You have teams of people who have worked longer hours for no extra pay and feel that they "deserve" something more for their efforts.

In short, the conditions are fertile for ethical infractions in many companies.

As the business leader, how do you ensure that your solid ethics and high integrity infiltrate your organization completely, thus minimizing the risk of ethical violations?

First, I will tell you what **not** to do. Do not do what every company does. Do not bring in a consultant or a canned program discussing ethics and integrity and have everyone be forced to sit through the program and answer 10 ridiculously simple questions that Bernie Madoff could answer correctly blind-folded. This wastes time and insults your employees with virtually no impact other than ensuring that you can say that you have an ethics program.

To have ethics and integrity permeate every fiber and every sinew of your business, consider the following:

1. Set the example

2. Regularly talk about ethics and ethical situations

3. Be aggressive in chasing down ethical violations and then air this dirty laundry

Set the Example of Ethics and Integrity

By now, you probably could guess that setting the example as the leader was going to be one of the three key points.

It is vitally important that you are ethical, and it is vitally important that you are seen to be ethical. That means not involving yourself in any situation that is or may appear to be unethical or inappropriate.

Of course, this applies to the big and obvious ethical violations such as criminal activity, taking bribes, kick-backs, collusion,

> *"Principled leaders must make a difference in the world. To be a principled leader, a person must have many skills and qualities, including the highest standards of integrity, sound judgment, and a strong moral compass — an intuitive sense of what is right and wrong."*
>
> **Kim Clark, Dean of Harvard Business School**

or price fixing. As a leader, you cannot even go near any of these things being especially careful about conversations that you may have with leaders of competitor companies at trade shows or trade association meetings. Further, be attuned to the risk to your reputation found in the gray area of such things as favoritism, nepotism or excessive entertainment or gift-giving.

Finally, be seen setting the correct example in small things. Yes, you are the leader of the company, but... Do not take office supplies and bring them home. Do not use tools or any other items for your personal use. Do not treat yourself to special breaks that are not available to others. Be especially aware on all your expense reports that you pay for everything that could appear to be personal or explain why they are bona fide business expenses. Yes, bookkeepers and accountants are not supposed to talk, however... In short, every small ethical transgression eats away at the fabric of what you are preaching.

Be ethical and be seen to be ethical in all things, big or small, black, white or gray. Enough said.

Regularly Talk about Ethics and Ethical Situations

This is easier than you think. When you attend meetings, have training sessions or have brown bag lunch sessions, bring up ethical situations that you or others in the company may have seen. Make sure that they are relevant to what the employees might experience at the office or factory. Invite five to ten minutes of roundtable discussions. No more. And repeat on a regular basis.

Over time, it will be more powerful if others in the group discuss ethical situations that they have encountered. By having these discussions, you lay down the ethical framework that you and your leadership team want and you will often set policy for certain types of ethical situations that you may not have considered before.

Some discussions points:

- A supervisor in the plant borrows tools over the weekend to do a personal task.
- A salesman exaggerates and embellishes his expense report.
- An employee in the plant sees broken items in the trash that he can fix and takes them home.
- Unethical incidences at sister companies.
- Unethical incidences at other companies that you may have heard or read about.

The key in all of this is the example, the discussion, and you or your top management team driving home the ethical issues.

I can hear some of you thinking. Wait a minute! An employee in the plant takes home some broken items that he found in the trash. That is not an ethical violation. Perhaps, but where do you draw the line?

> At one plant, employees would systematically throw away perfectly good electrical components. They would throw them into one waste bucket which they would always insist upon emptying themselves. At the end of the day, they would take out the "broken" components, bring them home and re-sell them.

To me, this is clearly unethical behavior. And when it was discovered, the employees in question were terminated. By bringing up these examples and discussing what is acceptable and what is not acceptable you will clarify and narrow the boundaries of the "gray area" and reinforce the high level of ethics that you require in your business.

Be Aggressive in Chasing Down Ethical Violations and Then Air this Dirty Laundry

In the past, I have personally failed on aggressively chasing down ethical violations.

> Several years ago, there was a good employee reasonably high up in a very successful and profitable business unit. The individual was, to my view at the time, devoted to the company and was definitely a workaholic, travelling 3½ weeks a month. Some discrepancies appeared in spending with his credit card. We immediately confronted him. He denied everything offering an excuse that stretched the boundary of credibility, but could have happened. We believed him and did not dig any further...

By now, you can imagine the rest of the story.

> Several months later, other discrepancies came to light, we finally decided to investigate in depth, and it was revealed that this individual had used company funds to buy personal items. Once this was determined, we acted immediately, and the individual was terminated. The monetary amount was not that high —less than $10,000. But, the damage to our reputation was much higher. This person, by virtue of his senior role, was, in the customer's eyes, a reflection of our company. As a result, both suppliers and customers thought that this business unit lacked high ethical standards.

The lessons learned are ample:

1. Without pre-judging, where there is smoke there is usually fire. So, seek it out.

2. When you find out about something, it has usually been going on for a long time and is a whole lot worse than you first thought.

3. Any employee's lack of ethics represents, in the minds of outside stakeholders, a lack of ethics of the company.

The fourth point that we learned is that you need to air the dirty laundry about these incidents. For legal or other reasons, most companies sweep such events under the rug and they are only known through the "rumor channel." Don't do that. As we did in this situation, explain what happened (you can do this in vague enough terms to please your corporate lawyers or human resources department), explain how it went wrong, explain what you did wrong, explain the lack of controls that have now been fixed, and explain how you will act differently in the future.

> *"The supreme quality of leadership is unquestionably integrity. Without it, no real success is possible no matter whether it is on a section gang, a football field, in an army, or in an office."*
>
> **President Dwight D. Eisenhower**

Your *mea culpa* ("I'm guilty!!") is difficult and embarrassing; you expose your weaknesses and mistakes to your team and the organization. But, by doing this, you really show your strength, your leadership, and your commitment to ethics and integrity.

In summary, the character, ethics and integrity of you and your entire team are really the bedrock upon which your business success is built.

- Financially, you want ethical people in your organization to be your eyes and ears to ensure that others do not steal or defraud and to communicate that fact upward if it happens.

- Legally, an ethical organization is much less vulnerable to lawsuits and retribution.
- Ethical employees want to work with ethical employees. You, as the leader, may be the most ethical person in the world. But, if an employee's immediate supervisor is not, then, in that employee's mind, you and the organization are unethical and potentially corrupt.
- Customers assume, rightly or wrongly, that any unethical act by an employee has the blessing and support of higher management. When the customer is aware of the unethical act, it is, of course, obvious to them. Thus, they think that it should be obvious to everyone in management at the organization. Ergo, the organization is unethical.

Only by doing the tough and right things of setting an example, maintaining the discussion, and aggressively chasing down and then publicizing transgressions will you bring your high values in ethics and integrity to life for you and your entire organization.

CHAPTER 11 – BE HONEST...
REALLY BE HONEST

"Honesty is the first chapter in the book of wisdom."

Thomas Jefferson

- *The importance of candor*
- *Creating a culture of honesty*
- *Be honest with the customer*

The Importance of Candor

Honesty has a number of synonyms: truth, candor, "face reality." Despite the many different words, honesty is not common enough in the business world. As Jack Welch writes:

Lack of candor is the biggest dirty little secret in business.

In business today...
- Companies are not honest and frank about the performance of the company.
- Managers are not candid in their performance evaluations.
- Leaders and employees are often not honest with themselves.

This lack of honesty is so pervasive that we just expect a lack of candor and white lies and are surprised when someone is blatantly honest.

Consider this fictional excerpt from a quarterly earnings statement that you and I will never read:

> Today, Acme Corporation announces a 25% increase in earnings year over year. This increase exceeds the analyst projections and entitles me to the full complement of my bonus. But, it is not a great thing for the company and let me tell you why. In short, despite the increase, we did not have a good quarter.
>
> - First, the economy was just stronger than anyone had expected. So, demand was higher and we rode that to improved sales despite continuing to lose market share.
> - Second, the weather was perfect. We had screwed up and over-stocked on swimwear for the summer, but warmer than expected weather throughout September and October on the West Coast and in the South helped us move those items. Moreover, on the East Coast, it was much colder than expected so we got a great head start on selling out our Winter line.
> - Third, the charge that we took last year when we were really sucking wind was, of course, much too high so we were able to write some of that back to profit.
> - Finally, as I am 65 and retiring soon, we have continued our aggressive program of eating our seed corn and being focused on the short term. Product development and marketing expenses remain below the appropriate level to grow the business and our market share continues its steady decline.
>
> In short, we made our numbers. But, we really are not as good as you give us credit for.

The beauty of honesty and candor is that it highlights what needs to be done for all to see. In the above example, Acme Corporation would know the critical issues that it needs to focus on: its demand forecasting and inventory management; its decline in market share; and its weak product development pipeline.

> *To paraphrase Warren Buffett, honesty and candor allows everyone to clearly see "who is swimming naked."*

Alas, when a company issues its typically less than candid press release blaming poor weather or lower than expected demand, the critical issues of the business are allowed to remain invisible. No one is facing reality.

Creating a Culture of Honesty

You engrain honesty in your company in the same way as you engrain ethics and integrity: you lead by example, publicize failures and the lessons learned, and look gift horses in the mouth.

<u>Lead By Example</u>

No surprise here; the leader needs to set the example in the case of honesty and candor.

- *Be Humble*

    One of the most difficult challenges for any leader is to remain humble in light of the success that the leader has achieved. Humility is the personal honesty that you, as the leader, do not

    > *"To possess self-confidence and humility at the same time is called maturity."*
    >
    > **Jack Welch**

    know everything and do not have all the answers. Humility enables you to question people's flattery, to admit your mistakes and weaknesses, and to be more open to other's opinions and challenges to your viewpoints. It is not a coincidence that in *Good to Great*, Jim Collins identifies the characteristics of the best leaders as possessing:

> A paradoxical blend of personal humility and professional will.

• *Admit Mistakes*

For your team, the most obvious sign of your humility will be your ability to admit that you made mistakes.

> When I taught classes to my team about the importance of honesty, I would stop and ask a quick question. "Today, in this class, we have a special visitor. We have the person who in this entire business division has made the biggest and most expensive mistakes. Try to guess which one of us it is." It would inevitably take about a minute or two before someone would gather up the courage to ask if I was speaking about myself. Of course, as the head of the business division, I had made the biggest decisions and thus had made the biggest mistakes.

My favorite episode of the 1970's sitcom, *Happy Days*, involves the Fonz and his inability to admit that he made a mistake. Throughout the episode, Fonzie tries to say that he was wrong.

> *"I may have many faults, but being wrong is not one of them."*
>
> **Jimmy Hoffa**

All that comes out of his mouth is: "I was wrrrr. I was wrrrr."

As leaders, many of us are like the Fonz. We just cannot admit that we made a mistake, even when it is obvious to everyone within the organization that we have done so. We make excuses. We pass the buck. We refuse to express regret. In short, we exhibit all the behaviors that limit us as leaders and weaken our standing among our employees.

- *Admit That You Don't Know*

    Another leadership weakness is refusing to admit that we don't know. Like many others, I have certainly suffered from this annoying habit. In many cases, this bravado may come from a lack of confidence and insecurity:

    > We are leaders. We know and understand the big picture.
    > We know and understand everything about our business. We
    > are leaders.

    But, admitting that you don't know is vital. Because it makes it possible for others in the organization to admit that they don't know. This improves the candor and the honesty and prevents de-moralizing situations that I have seen where you truly have the blind (people who don't know what they are doing) leading the sighted.

    A few years ago, I asked a question of one of my stronger, but still learning, General Managers. His honest response was totally disarming:

    > David, I do not know the answer. In fact, I do not even know
    > where to begin to lie.

- *Refuse to Speak and Accept BS*

    Noble Prize Winning Physicist Richard Feynman had it right when he said:

    > The first principle is that you must not fool yourself, and you
    > are the easiest person to fool.

    In short, speak the truth as best as you know it or say nothing at all. All of us as people, leaders, and employees have very astute BS detectors. We just are not fooling anyone by speaking or letting someone get away with speaking BS.

The more insidious result from speaking and accepting BS is that we may lose touch with reality.

You will often see this happen in failing companies where the leaders and employees believe sincerely that they are performing well, even heroically. They have accepted the BS so long that they do not know what is up and what is down. To change this mindset will then require a cold bath of "Face Reality." Avoid the shivering and start requiring the truth, painful and ugly as it can be.

Our astute BS detectors, however, often fail us when it comes to receiving flattery. In a recent experiment, psychologists tried to determine at what level flattery of a leader by a subordinate became just too much and had a negative effect. The conclusion of the experiment was that when done right, there was no negative effect to flattering the leader, no matter how much flattery was done. Of course, this was just one scientific experiment. But it should give us pause. While we all grow frustrated with the obvious brown-noser, we still need to be especially attuned to the flattery of others that report to us. We don't want to begin believing

> *Surrounded by sycophants at court, French King "Louis XIV's greatest gift was to maintain his quality of common sense in the midst of constant flattery."*
>
> **Louis XIV Biographer, Olivier Bernier**

our glowing press releases. We want to recognize and reject the BS of flattery.

• *Be Candid in Performance Reviews*

When I have acquired or taken over a business, I often begin by reading everyone's performance reviews. As such, I am whisked back to Lake Wobegon, Minnesota. Lake Wobegon is the fictional town of radio personality Garrison Keillor where:

All the women are strong, all the men are good looking, and all the children are above average.

It is surprising how an organization can fail while all of its employees are receiving "above expectations" and "superior ratings" in their performance reviews.

This is something to avoid. So begin to be honest in your performance reviews. Knowing and pointing out someone's weaknesses is vital as their manager. It may mean that they need to work hard to improve on the weaknesses. It may mean that they need some help and a re-definition of their job responsibilities to focus on their strengths while someone else covers for their weaknesses. It may mean that they are a wrong fit for the job. But, it definitely means that the weaknesses need to be addressed and spoken about.

Publicize Failures and the Lessons Learned

If you have lead by example in being honest, then publicizing failures in your company will come naturally. Moreover, developing lessons learned from these failures, even if only a one page, five bullet point list is invaluable for organizational learning.

> "When you lose, don't lose the lesson."
>
> **Dalai Lama**

Many successful companies conduct post-mortems on all their major projects, initiatives, and acquisitions, both the successes and the failures. These post-mortems are then disseminated and become a source of learning and continuous improvement.

- What went well?
- What went wrong? What could we have done better to detect earlier what went wrong? What could we have done better to correct what went wrong?

The answers do not need to be very long. In fact, it is better if they are kept to three to five points. But, these lessons learned will be productive the next time your company tries to do something similar.

Look Gift Horses in the Mouth

As my fictional quarterly earnings statements attests, it is the rare company that analyzes what goes right and why. For most companies and leaders [I have been guilty of this], the common response is: "You have made your numbers. Great job." But, dig deeper to ensure that the performance was really excellent and to determine whether critical issues in the business may have changed.

- Sales are up. But, are we losing market share?
- Profits are up. But, are we continuing to invest in new product and market development?
- Cash flow is strong. But, is our business declining?

To understand the reality and be honest, focus on and question the good parts of the results as well as the bad parts.

Be Honest with the Customer

In Section V, we will discuss customer service in more detail. One of the pillars of effective customer service is telling the truth and being honest with the customer, especially when a mistake has been made or there is a delay.

As the supplier to the customer, this lack of honesty comes from the fear of losing the customer because of the mistake.

Yet, if we think of ourselves as a customer, we would likely respect a company that is promptly honest with us and admits its mistakes Further, by being honest, this company would help us mitigate the effects and cost of the mistake or delay. Second, this company would certainly stand out from the crowd as it is so rare for companies to give their customers direct, punctual and frank answers.

The importance of being forthright and honest with the customer was a lesson that I learned the hard way.

In the midst of one turnaround, the business was experiencing significant quality and delivery issues with multiple customers. All of us were living in fear of losing the customers, so we did not tell any of them about the impending delays. With one of the larger customers, the delivery was delayed and, as a result, the customer's project was delayed. Due to their project's delay, the project managers on the customer side (who had an influence in choosing vendors) each personally lost a few thousand dollars in bonus money at the end of the year. The terse response back from the key customer contact sticks in my head anytime that I, or anyone on my team, consider being less than forthright and honest to a customer:

> Had all parties known of the delays, we may not have been happy but at least we would have had an opportunity to make planned adjustments to schedule and revenue. And we could have avoided the negative personal financial consequences which resulted.

As you may imagine, it was a hard, multi-year slog to win back the trust and business of this customer.

CHAPTER 12 – SEEK OUT THE "TRUE TRUTH"

> "Men occasionally stumble over the truth, but most of them pick themselves up and hurry off as if nothing ever happened."
>
> Sir Winston Churchill

- *Seek out Multiple Viewpoints*
- *Listen*
- *Observe*

To create an ethical and honest culture in an organization, seek out and find the "true truth" and thus make decisions based on facts rather than opinions.

On July 12, 1998, Brazil lost to France in the World Cup final by a score of 3 - 0.[3] Earlier in the day, Ronaldo, Brazil's star and the best player in the world at the time, had suffered a seizure of some type. In any event, he played the game, but played poorly. After the game, the Brazilian public and media could not believe that their favorites had lost. This led to a suspicion of foul play and corruption. The Brazilian senate decided to investigate the event and determine why

---

3   This story comes from the book, <u>Futebol: The Brazilian Way of Life</u>, by Alex Bellos, Bloomsbury Publishing: Great Britain, 2002.

Brazil had lost. Ronaldo was, quite naturally, called to testify. He gave his opening remarks:

> I also hope that my truth pleases you, because there are many truths, many truths. It's up to you [the Brazilian Senate Commission] to decide which is the true truth and analyze it afterwards.

"My truth." "The true truth."

For our purposes of business leadership, Ronaldo hit the nail on the head. As a leader, it is your job to seek out and find the true truth. You will hear lots of truths from lots of different people. You may call it their opinions, but to them it is not their opinions, it is the truth. It is their truth. As a leader, you will need to listen to all these "truths" to determine the "true truth", the "real reality."

> *"There are three sides to every story; your side, my side, and the truth. And no one is lying."*
>
> **Robert Evans,**
> **Hollywood Producer**

To find this "true truth", seek out multiple viewpoints, listen and observe.

Seek Out Multiple Viewpoints

This one should be easy, but it is not. Be a researcher and a historian. Get the primary source material from the mouths of your customers and employees. This means direct engagement with the customer. This means developing relationships with people in your business below your direct reports. This means listening to other stakeholders.

Further, in any issue, dispute, or conflict, get the viewpoints of all sides.

I would tell my General Managers that I would never fault them for making a wrong decision after getting the "truths" from all key stakeholders. But, I would fault them for not getting the "truths" from all affected stakeholders, even if they made the right decision in the end.

Listen

Listening is one of those skills where 90% of us rate ourselves as being in the top 10%. Alas, most of us (including me) do not listen well. As evidenced by this quote from Sir Francis Bacon, the advice on how to listen well has been the same for at least four hundred years:

Listen not to contradict and disprove, nor to believe and take for granted, nor to find talk and discourse, but to weigh and consider.

We all know how to listen well; we just do not do it. Some simple ideas to try include:

- **Physically force yourself not to be distracted**. Move away from the desk and keyboard, put down the smart phone, remove the distraction, look in the person's eyes and listen.
- **Pause before replying** to ensure that you understood everything that was said. If you need a little trick to help you actually do that, then count to three (in your mind) before responding.
- **Briefly summarize what the other person has just said.**
- Especially for meetings, **create an "interruption fund"** where you pay $5 for a quarter-end group lunch anytime someone interrupts.

I have one anecdote about interrupting to share.

Early in my career, I had an excellent mentor. During one meeting, I proceeded to interrupt him. He told me that I was interrupting him.

> So, of course, I interrupted him to tell him why I interrupt so much. His response was to interrupt me and tell me the following:

>> I don't care why you interrupt because I don't care about the "why." It took me thirty years of psychoanalysis to realize that the "why" does not matter. What matters is to just not do it. So, do not do it. Do not interrupt.

Another aspect of listening is to listen to and interpret the meaning behind the words. Most of us make the assumption (which is usually the case) that people are telling us the truth. But, they are always telling us "their truth." We must first respect that it is their truth; that it is what they believe. In addition, however, we must think about and reflect on their point of view and why they are saying what they are saying.

In his book *The Management Myth,* Matthew Stewart describes the listening style of one quite brilliant consultant as follows:

> He does not focus on what you are saying. Rather, he tries to figure out what you want to get by saying it. And then he tries to figure out why you think you want what you want. And then he tries to figure out what he can do about the things that make you think you want it.

This consultant's "third order" listening skills may be a little too deep for all of us. But, as a leader, trying to 'figure out what the other person wants to get by saying something' is sage advice.

Observe

Get out there and carefully observe the reality as it really is, not as you want it to be. Most top executives are treated to Potemkin Villages when they go out and see the businesses they oversee.

The expression "Potemkin Village" comes from Russia in the late 1700's. According to this story, a Russian minister, Potemkin, wanted to impress the Empress Catherine II during a state visit. So, he had hollow facades of villages constructed along the barren banks of the Dnieper River to impress Empress Catherine the Great as her boat sailed down the river.

In both my previous companies, any announced visit by a top executive, a member of the Board of Directors, or a group of Wall Street analysts would result in a two week spruce up campaign on the facility sometimes to the tune of $30,000 or more. Having approved these expenditures on numerous occasions, I find it hard to fault anyone in the field for initiating such a spruce-up effort. But, the reality is that the top executives are not seeing the company as it really exists.

As a leader, it is your job to side-step the spruce up campaign and look behind the façades of the Potemkin Village to observe what the business is like on a normal day. This can involve regular visits or surprise visits or just looking closely in the corners or under the covers.

As an anecdote that encompasses all aspects of seeking out the "true truth," I relate a sales call I made as a sales manager a number of years ago.

> I often traveled with my salespeople to observe them in action and to interact with the customer. In the sales calls, I knew that my presence changed everything. When I was with the salespeople, they were on their game, organized, prepared, and with pressed shirts. The purpose of my sales management calls was to get the customer's point of view and to see how the salespeople performed when they were at their best. I could usually accomplish these two objectives. What I could not usually get was the truth in how the sales people were on their normal days.
>
> But on this sales call, I found out.

I was with a salesperson and he was asking the right questions, listening carefully, and generally putting on a good show. He was on his game, and I was impressed. The customer was engaged and asking good, if a little bit basic, questions. And the customer had a big smile on his face the entire time that the salesperson was presenting. In any event, as the sales call wound down, the salesperson had to get something from his car, so I was left alone with the customer. Not being the shy and retiring type, I asked the customer about the basic questions he was asking and his smile. His response:

> Please don't tell Ken (I changed the name), but I am smiling because I am really impressed with how well he can present and sell when he has to, and I am asking these questions because we have never really talked about most of this stuff before. Usually, Ken just comes in, we go immediately to lunch, have a pleasant non-business conversation, and he leaves.

Ouch! Despite the odd bout of pain, it always pays to seek out and find the true truth.

In summary, only when the reality is correctly determined and understood, can your business identify the right critical issues and make the correct decisions. To determine the real reality or identify the root problem, you must first seek out and find the "true truth."

Finally, I thought that you might like to know. In December 2001, the Brazilian Senate Commission published its findings about what happened at the 1998 World Cup Final. Their conclusion about Brazil was that "we lost because we did not win."

Chapter 13 – Determine Your Values and Goals

"The industrial landscape is already littered with the remains of once successful companies that could not adapt their strategic vision to altered conditions."

Ralph Abernathy

- *Why Not Vision?*
- *Values*
- *Goals*

As the leader of your company, you need to create and communicate a clear image of how your company will conduct its business (the values) and what it hopes to achieve (the goals).

Why Not Vision?

Many business leaders and management thinkers lump the concepts of values, goals and direction together under the word "vision". I, however, avoid using this word. First, the word "vision" has been so over-used and so misused that it has truly lost all meaning. Second, most companies would struggle to come up with a singular vision which incorporates even 80% of what they do. Yes, start-ups, small, focused companies or even larger single market companies can have a unified vision. But, most mid-sized to large companies serve multiple markets and have several product lines. In such cases, one overall vision cannot be applied to the whole business without being empty words.

> For my division, each of the companies (and even parts of each company) focused on different markets with different product lines. As such, it was impossible to create a singular vision. The best that we came up with, while accurate, was neither inspiring nor useful:

>> To be the leading manufacturing and services company to the customers we want to serve in the markets we want to serve in the geographic areas we are focused on.

Third, a vision should be longer-term, even permanent. But, the business reality changes so much that any vision would need to change at least every three years, if not every year. As such, I believe that having well-communicated and concrete business goals are more useful than having an abstract company vision or mission statement.

Values

While most of your business goals will become obsolete within three years, your values need to endure. As the leader, it is your job to determine and communi-cate the values that you want to permeate your business. If you are a profit center in a larger business, your values will certainly need to be in general agreement with the values of the larger corporation.

> *"Throughout history, the mark of an enduring civilization has been that it has a common set of shared values."*
>
> **Professor Rufus Fears**

Otherwise, you will experience the stress and tension that I faced (Chapter 2) as the values of the parent company that I worked for moved away from my values.

The values need to come from within you.

- What do you hold dear?
- What do you consider most important?
- How do you like to see business conducted?

By the time that you have gotten to a leadership role you have doubtless thought about your values quite a good deal. Initially, you will come up with at least ten values that are critical. Write them down. Ask other people in your company about them. Ask your family and friends about them.

Then, whittle this list down to the most important three values. Three is ideal; but, up to five is acceptable. With any more than five, you will have no way to communicate them to your team and have them be remembered and be kept front of mind.

It is likely that you have seen or read dozens of corporate vision statements that contain a laundry list of company values. Alas, it would be nearly impossible to remember them, let alone to communicate them and have everyone in the company really live by them.

In the last two months alone, I have seen corporate value statements prominently displayed on two of the companies that I have done business with. One had ten values listed; the other had fifteen. Do you really believe that anyone in the company can remember all of these values, let alone actively think about them and apply them in their day to day work?

When younger, I was a Boy Scout. The Boy Scouts do a great job of getting you to remember the Boy Scout Law with the twelve values of a Boy Scout: trustworthy, loyal… In fact, I can still recite the list more than 30 years later. The values are excellent and relevant, but there are just too many of them to keep front of mind and use daily. More often, you would be reminded of the values after the fact when

you did not live up to them: "David, what you did was not very thrifty,
now was it?"

Even with the years that I have been preaching, teaching, coaching and training on the three values for my companies (do the right
thing, winning teamwork, customer service), it has remained a daily
challenge to communicate them and have them "stick" in employee's
minds.

But, why do values matter?

- Shared values are the essential element to create the culture
  of the business and the way of doing things that allows for
  alignment, for having everyone row in the same direction.
- Values matter because it is not only achieving the strategic
  goals that matters to a successful leader, it is how they are achieved.

  > "When it comes to bringing values to life —
  > to doing the good, right, and appropriate
  > thing...we're always working at it, we're
  > never totally there, and the challenge starts
  > all over again with each new tomorrow."
  >
  > **Eric Harvey and Steve Ventura**

- Shared values become a lens through
  which all decisions can be made and can be judged. In my
  companies, any decision that is made should not violate the
  ethic of doing the right thing, should not be detrimental to
  developing a winning team, and should not be counter to
  building a portfolio of satisfied customers.

In short, values matter and you need to communicate them. If
you want, use mine as a starting point and then refine as you see
fit to match your own personal values and the values that are most
important for the success of the business that you are leading.

Goals

Once you have refined your values and begun to communicate them, the values need to be permanent. Changing and continually refining the values leads to confusion and misalignment. By contrast, your business goals will change over time as the critical issues the business faces change.

To determine the goals and strategies of your business, you must first understand the reality and the opportunities in the business, then determine the critical issues, then flesh out and focus on three business goals.

Understand the Business Reality and the Opportunities

To be relevant, the goals of the business need to reflect the business reality and the opportunities that the business faces. For years, businesses have used SWOT analyses to understand the competitive reality and opportunities for businesses. SWOT stands for strengths, weaknesses, opportunities and threats. In theory, a SWOT analysis is a good way to understand the business reality. In practice, however, a SWOT analysis is usually just a superficial re-tread of ideas done quickly to fill out the required Power Point slide for the budget or strategic plan presentation. Rarely have I seen the level of analysis needed to make it meaningful and useful.

To ensure that you understand the reality and see the "true" truth of your business situation, you need to get fresh eyes, dig deep to get the facts, and determine the Mokitas.

• *Get Fresh Eyes*

The first step is for both you and your key leadership team to take a step back from the day to day activity and look at the bigger picture. See the forest for the trees.

Some suggestions:

> • **Take time away from the office, untethered**. Go on vacation or take a full-week class somewhere. Getting

away serves two purposes. First, you will see your team in action without you. Is your team strong enough to handle the business while you are gone? Who steps up while you are gone to lead the business? What problems occur? Why? Are you so important to the business that the business begins to fail without you? Are you the problem in the business (dictator, micro-manager, etc.)? Second, you gain a perspective on the business that you will likely have missed while fighting the daily battles. Instead of operating at 10,000 feet, you get the chance to fly up and see the business at 35,000 feet and look at the bigger picture.

- **Mix things up.** Require key leadership team members to swap roles for a few days. Get the Sales Vice President to spend time on the plant floor; have the Operations Vice President go on customer calls; and have Operations Managers visit each other's operations. They each will get a broadened perspective and have some insight into the other's area of expertise.

- **If you can, "eat your own dog food."** Be a customer and see what the customer experience is like. Be a customer (or get an associate to be a customer) of your top competitor to see what that customer experience is like.

> The turn-key services business that we started gave us the chance to see the world through the eyes of our customer. The services business would buy product from a plant, install, complete assembly and outfitting, be responsible for final testing, and provide on-going maintenance. The feedback that we got from this group was priceless as we realized all the hassles and issues that we caused the customer by having 98% quality. When the services business purchased from competitors the quality was often

better than what we provided, and they were much easier
to do business with. By getting this customer experience,
we were able to see the brutal facts about our quality and
service and thus improve them.

- *Dig Deep to Get the Facts*

The next step is to get the data to fully understand the state of
the company, the competitive reality, and the market opportunities.

- **Spend some time with your customers and suppliers.**
  Learn their businesses and understand what is happening
  in their industries. What can you do better in serving
  your customers? Where else can you help them in improving their business? What opportunities do they see?
- **Listen to employees throughout your company.** Get out
  of the office and speak with employees on the front line
  of the business, managers in the level below your direct
  reports, salespeople. Ask them about their priorities and
  challenges. Determine their understanding of the values
  and goals of the business. Get a sense of their motivation
  and morale. Ask them about opportunities for improvement or growth that they see.
- **Read and listen to what others say about your company.**
  Review customer satisfaction surveys. Read customer
  letters. Keep tabs on your company on Social Media
  including Facebook and Twitter. Google your company
  and set up a Google alert. See what is being written or
  said about the company, if anything.
- **Follow your industry, competitors, customers and their
  industry.** Keep tabs in the press and on Social Media.
  Read their Websites.
- **Get additional viewpoints.** Get the viewpoint of your
  board or your boss. Invite a trusted mentor, confidant,
  or business associate to come in and see the business and

give their views. Speak with bankers and even Wall Street analysts if your industry is covered by them.

- **Do a formal competitive analysis.** Get a number of key individuals in the company to do a modified Porter Five Forces (see Chapter 25) analysis of the business, evaluating the company's relative competitive position.

The key word in all of these points is **listening.** By making a concentrated effort to get your key leadership team out of the office, interacting with, and listening to employees, customers and other stakeholders, you will learn more about the strengths and weaknesses of your team, your customers, and your competitive situation. You will also be educating and broadening the perspectives of your leadership team. And you will likely increase morale because people suddenly feel as if they are being heard. As Brian Dunn, CEO of Best Buy, has said:

> One of my roles as CEO is to be the chief listener. I don't believe that the model is any longer that there are a few really smart people at the top of the pyramid that make all the strategic decisions. It is much more about being all around the enterprise, and looking for people with great ideas and passionate points of view that are anchored to the business and connected to things our customers care about.

- *Determine the Mokitas*

At this stage you are likely confident that you understand well the business reality. Before moving on, we need to dig a little deeper and get a few more pieces of data.

- Write down the three most significant Mokitas in your company.

What?!? Huh?!? What the $*#)% is a Mokita? According to Wikipedia, Mokita is a term from Papua New Guinea which describes:

> The truth we all know but agree not to talk about.

Your Mokitas are the dirty little secrets in your company that are really not so secret. Some possible Mokitas:

- We have other business, but all of our profit comes from sales to one customer.
- The industry we serve is going into decline and will never come back.
- As a leader, I am the 'Genius with a Thousand Helpers.' I am so important to the company. They could not do anything without me.
- My heart is just not in the business any more. But I do not know what else to do.
- Our customers think we are arrogant and hate us. But, they buy from us only because everyone else is worse.
- In order to get ahead in this company, you have to have the right last name.
- My operations manager makes his numbers, but he is really a jerk and everyone who works for him hates him.
- My sales manager really wants to do sales and does not know how to manage; he took the management job just to get a promotion and more money.
- For the past several years, we have needed to focus on sales, but everybody in the organization came up through finance and operations. And nobody wants or even likes to do sales.

> *"Most companies explain away the brutal facts rather than having to confront the brutal facts head-on."*
>
> **The Oz Principle**

Every business has at least one, if not two or three Mokitas. In forcing yourself to find the Mokitas in your company, you are asking the really tough questions that need to be asked to determine the brutal facts.

I can hear you thinking: my team does not have the time to do all this!

First, as always, the 80/20 rule applies. A lot can be accomplished with just 20% of the effort. Think about how much value you could get from a single overnight trip for the Vice President of Operations to visit with four customers. Second, for you as a leader, determining the true picture of the business reality should be a priority. It is far better that this effort be led and completed by the leader and his leadership team than having it be out-sourced to a strategy consulting firm who will do the exact same fact-finding and analysis for a pretty penny.

Determine the Critical Issues

At this stage, you are
likely to be overwhelmed
with issues and opportu-
nities. The objective now
is to determine the three
most important. In this
phase, it is all about deter-

> *"Focusing on the right critical issues —
> no more, than three to five, in most
> cases — is crucial to achieving success."*
>
> *Lessons from Private Equity any
> Company Can Use*

mining what is most critical for the success of the business.

You may have to repeat this stage more than once. The first time
around you may come up with ten critical issues and opportunities.
But you will have to whittle the list down further. Three is ideal; but
any more than five issues and opportunities will dilute your focus
too much.

Keep the list of the critical issues that are whittled away. When
the most important three issues have been resolved or the opportunity
realized, the other issues may then be considered if they still represent
a critical issue at that stage of your company's progress.

As you analyze your data and debate with your team about the
problems, issues, and opportunities you will want to consider...

* *Focus on Root Cause*

If you are looking to determine a problem or critical issue, use
Toyota's concept of the **"Five Whys"** to ensure that you are focusing
on the root cause of the problem rather than a symptom. In using
the "Five Whys" to address a problem, you start with a why question, to every answer ask a why question, repeat five times and you
will usually come to the underlying cause of the problem which is
what needs to be solved.

One of our businesses had poor delivery reliability. At first, the issue
was defined as "need to improve delivery reliability." That helped no
one. By using the "Five Whys", it was determined that the problem
had actually nothing to do with production. The real issue was that
the project managers wanted to be as efficient as possible and enter

their orders in the system all at once. So, they did not enter the orders until they had all the final details resolved, which could take a few weeks. This then delayed purchasing from ordering long-lead time items, which delayed receipt of the items, which delayed production, which delayed the delivery of the product.

The only way to solve a problem is at its root. In this case, the problem was quite easily solved by a small change in the procedures used by project managers.

> *The success of Toyota's management principles comes from spending relatively more time and effort on defining the problem and critical issues and relatively less time on finding solutions.*

I offer another more expensive example:

In my time, I have seen a number of requests for major capital expenditure to solve an urgent production problem. Several times, these requests have been approved, and the equipment was purchased. Yet the urgent problem remained unsolved. In doing the post-mortem, it was determined that the expenditure was never needed. The root cause of the problem was poor leadership and poor execution that had never been and still was not being dealt with directly. These situations were costly and time-consuming wastes because we had not focused on the root cause. To top it all off, once we had the proper leadership in place, the newly purchased equipment often turned out to be irrelevant and was put to the side to rust and collect dust.

- *Focus on the Constraint*

The Theory of Constraints was proposed by Eliyahu Goldratt in his book, *The Goal*. This theory focuses on how to improve a production process by identifying and focusing on the constraint in the production system. The constraint is the bottleneck; it is what is holding the production system back from increasing throughput (output) and improving. Goldratt's view is that a relentless focus on the constraint is critical in improving the production system. Once that one constraint is improved, it is necessary to repeat the process and identify the new constraint.

> In one facility, we determined that the constraint was the overhead crane that was needed to lift and move product. Before spending significant money to buy a new crane, we re-scheduled production and workers' shifts so that the overhead crane never stopped; it was always lifting or moving product from the beginning of the workday to the end. As a result of this focus on the crane as the constraint, we were able to increase production throughput by 30% without any additional investment.

This concept directly applies to determining the critical issues of a business. What is the constraint in the business? What is holding the business back from being better? These are the most important issues that need to be addressed.

> An operational consultant colleague was invited into a production plant in central Pennsylvania to see what he could do to improve the operations further. The plant manager already had a number of initiatives under way and was genuinely open to new ideas. My friend was impressed; the plant was clean, well-laid out, and efficiently produced a quality product. Afterwards, he met with the President who was excited to know what more could be done to improve the plant. My colleague's answer was quite simple.

>> Don't do anything more in the plant. The plant runs very well. But, the most important thing that can be done to improve the business is to bring in more sales. Any tweaks and slight improvements in the plant would be minor compared to the improvements in the business with more sales.

In this case, the overall constraint (what is holding the business back) is not the plant, it is sales. By improving the plant further, you may make the plant better. But, that does not necessarily make the business better. It is great to have an excellent plant. But, the goal is not to have the best plant. The goal is to have the best overall business with the best competitive position. Thus, for this business, a critical issue would be to focus on improving sales.

- *Think of Wayne Gretzky*

Wayne Gretzky was arguably the greatest hockey player that ever lived. When asked for the key to his success in hockey he stated:

> A good hockey player plays where the puck is. I think about and play to where the puck is going to be.

In considering which opportunities are most important, consider whether you are aiming for where the market was, where the market is, or where the market is going to be. Are you looking to enter into a good, mature market or are you aiming for a currently small but growing market where you can develop a competitive advantage? No one builds lasting business success by being a late "me too" entrant in a mature market.

- *Think it Through*

Ask the following questions for each of the critical issues that you consider:

If we resolved this issue or realized this opportunity ...

- **What would this future look like**? How would we run the business? What skill sets would we need to have?
- **How much better would the business be**? Does the opportunity or improvement justify the effort?
- **Would we be able to sustain our differentiation and the competitive advantage**? Would we be properly organized to deliver better than the competition? Or would we just raise the cost of doing business for all supplier companies with all the benefit accruing to the customer? Would we

be competing against our current customers or current key suppliers?

This final exercise is a filter to ensure that you focus only on the critical issues, eliminating anything that does not drive your business forward in the direction that you want it to go. To do the right thing means to focus on what most needs to be done and only on what most needs to be done. Nothing else. As Peter Drucker said:

> There is surely nothing quite so useless as doing with great efficiency what should not be done at all.

Write out and Develop Three Goals for the Business

By knowing the few critical issues for the business, the goals will become apparent. In this stage, it is necessary to write out the goals and then to develop a one to two page goal plan for achieving each of the goals.

- *Brainstorm*

For each critical issue, brainstorm the solutions and action items that need to be accomplished to properly address the issue. The analysis done previously to determine the critical issues actually makes this step in the process a simple one. The goals will be obvious. And it will be easy to come up with a long list of solutions, ideas and action items. In doing this brainstorming, there are a few quick things to remember.

- **Do not re-invent the wheel**. If someone has a better idea, adapt and incorporate it. Legally plagiarize as much as possible; invention takes time and is expensive.
- **Remember the 80 / 20 rule**. 80% of the issues can be addressed by doing 20% of the activities that you have written down. Following this rule closely prevents you from focusing on trivial issues.
- **Build momentum**. Especially for difficult goals, choose a path where you can gain momentum over time. Pluck some low hanging (non-trivial) fruits first; think of

solving some easy problems to get some visible change and boost confidence. Continue to hit singles, not home runs.

- **Look at the time element.** Think critical path (see Chapter 16). Some action items may need to be started right now even if the solution cannot be implemented for a while.
- **You do not need to make everything perfect.** Again, think 80/100. Go for the 80% solution that is 100% implementable quickly rather than the perfect solution that is unlikely to be completed correctly and quickly.
- **Think of your team.** Make sure that you have the team in place capable of achieving the goal.

- *Determine the Three Goals*

After the brainstorming, it is necessary to set the three business goals in stone. The goals are set such that they can be accomplished in one to three years while addressing the critical issues and helping the business realize the biggest opportunities.

Once again, the challenge is to limit the number of goals to (ideally) three, but definitely no more than five. And to have the goals be balanced across the organization. As Peter Drucker and innumerable strategists have said:

> The biggest difficulty in business strategy is not deciding what to do; rather it is deciding what **not** to do.

Self-restraint is required to keep the list of goals to five or fewer. But, this discipline is essential. The purpose of creating goals is to move the business forward in a way that addresses the critical issues and opportunities faced by the business. Nothing is achieved if the goals are not achieved. With any more than three to five business goals, your chance of success diminishes rapidly. The leaders and employees who will be tasked to complete the goals cannot possibly focus on (let alone keep front of mind) that many goals and priorities. People just do not have the attention and perception span and the time.

> In every turnaround that we accomplished, we began by creating "Stop Doing" lists, as the failing business was trying to do too many things while accomplishing nothing.

> In another case that I have experience with, a struggling $20M business unit had 26 goals that it was working on at the same time.

Less is More. And any more than five goals is too much.

* *Write Down the Plan*

After determining the goals for the business, begin to write down and compile pages of ideas and action items about what is needed to realize each of the goals.

In my experience, these compilations can get quite lengthy; we often came up with eight pages worth. The next challenge is to whittle everything down to a one to two page game plan for each goal. This "play book" would list the overall business goal with detailed goals cascading from the overall goals with the name of the person assigned and the due date.

This is not exactly rocket science. As with everything about strategy, the real challenge is to whittle the list down and then **keep** it at two pages. Inevitably, some of the detailed goals will change or something new will need to be added. If this happens, it requires that something else be taken off the list to keep the goal plan to two pages and keep an overriding focus on the most important.

With three to five goals focused on the critical issues and the best opportunities and a detailed game plan for each goal, you are ready to align your team to achieve your goals and drive your business to success.

Think in Threes

*"In practice, a person should work on
three things at once, not forty."*

The Leadership Machine

- What is "Thinking in Threes?"
- Why "Think in Threes?"
- How to Apply "Thinking in Threes?"

In this book, you have seen me construct many lists to
clarify and explain. You have likely noted that most of these
lists have three points. In doing this, I am using a technique I
call "Thinking in Threes."

What is "Thinking in Threes?"

"Thinking in Threes" requires that you analyze, organize
and summarize most concepts and actions in three points.

In determining the three points, you strive to be MECE.
MECE is an analytical framework used by the management consulting company, McKinsey[4]; it stands for mutually exclusive and
collectively exhaustive. By mutually exclusive, you want to have
each of the three points stand on its own and be distinct from
the other two. By collectively exhaustive, you try to encompass
and explain the concept or action as completely as possible in
only the three points.

---

4   I am borrowing this concept of MECE from <u>The McKinsey Way</u> by
Ethan Rasiel.

But, you may say, many issues are complex and cannot be boiled down completely to three points. True, you may not catch all the nuances of the issue, but you will catch the gist and the most important points. In 98 out of 100 cases, if you accomplish the three most important points you will have achieved the goal.

Why Think in Threes?

First, thinking in threes requires you to do forced prioritization. It requires you to realize that having ten goals or ten action items means that most goals or items will not be done effectively. Having too many priorities does mean having no priorities, as companies rarely have the talent, energy, time, and attention span to accomplish more than three priorities. By Thinking in Threes, you are forced to prioritize on the most important three issues. These three issues can be kept front of mind and can then be more easily accomplished.

Second, thinking in threes improves the rigor and quality of your thinking. By forcing you to explain an issue in only three points, you can truly understand the issue and focus on the most important points. This enables you to put together an action plan that can then be communicated.

Third, thinking in threes significantly improves your ability to communicate and persuade. In the best of situations, listeners or readers can only grasp three to five points at a time. By having a clear, compact and succinct three points, communication can more easily take place and your team will be able to understand the issue and act on it. Further, you will be able to repeat and reiterate the three points and you will be able to follow-up on the three points. All this helps the three points to stick and remain in the front of your team members' minds.

As we will discuss in Chapter 17, effective communication is difficult even with three MECE points, let alone trying to communicate with an unfocused memo or speech that contains eight to twelve points or action items.

In the example in Chapter 8, the Divisional President colleague found no alignment in the production area between the priorities of the production worker and the priorities of each layer of management. Moreover, when he asked about the three most important priorities, none could give just three. Most had lists of priorities that were ten, twelve or fifteen items long and that often took five to ten minutes to recite. More tellingly, when asked to clarify, the list of priorities would change. As should be obvious by now, eight, ten, twelve, or fifteen priorities, goals, or values are impossible to keep straight and are impossible to live up to.

In this example, the General Manager could have set out three goals for production:

1. Safety and housekeeping of such high standard and so engrained in the culture that you would be happy to have your ten year old daughter wander around the plant by herself.

2. Every mistake is identified immediately and then the root cause is corrected.

3. Employees work with a sense of purpose and keep their commitments to the team.

While broad, these three goals could then be translated into specific actions down the line enabling everyone on the team to contribute in their own way to realizing the goals. These three goals would then be engrained in people's minds and remembered. These three goals would be able to be followed up and managed.

How to Apply "Thinking in Threes?"

The concept of "Thinking in Threes" can be applied throughout your business and even in your personal life.

1. Use in your written and spoken communication

2. As we have just seen, use in setting business and personal goals and priorities. What are the three critical issues for our business? What are the three goals for the overall business? What are the three specific goals for our area of the business?

3. Use in employee and leadership management. What are the three key things that you did well this year? What are the three challenges that you had this year? What are your three key improvement / development areas that need to be addressed in the next year?

In summary:

1. Keep things simple in a complex world.

2. Focus on and achieve the most important things that you set out to achieve.

3. Think in Threes!!!

Chapter 14 – Align the Organization to Your Values and Goals

"Leaders must build alignment around a new path forward. They must force extraordinary focus and consistency of purpose."

Mike Romley

- *Right People Doing the Right Job*
- *Translate the Goals of the Business into Three Specific Goals for Each Employee*
- *Explain the Goals. . .Teach the Values*

In the previous chapter, we discussed the importance of determining the values and the goals for the business. Once these have been determined, the challenge is to align the organization to focus on these values and goals. This is the final pillar to ensure that your business (and everyone in your business) focuses on doing the right things for the success of the business and only these right things.

To create this alignment, you will need to:

- Have the Right People Doing the Right Job
- Translate the Business Goals into Three Specific Goals for Each Employee
- Explain the Goals...Teach the Values

Right People Doing the Right Job

<u>Align the Leadership Team</u>

As discussed in Chapter 8, the first step is to ensure that the key leadership team fully supports the values and the business goals. Everyone on the leadership team needs to be rowing in the same direction. A key leader, even if successful, cannot be allowed to remain on the team if he does not fully support the leader's values and goals for the business. I know the importance of this first hand:

> As I have mentioned in my biography, I worked for Oldcastle for 16 years until early 2010. I had joined the company because of its fast-paced, non-bureaucratic culture and the opportunity to run a business as an entrepreneur with the support of a big company. In my ten years running a Division for Oldcastle Precast, I had success. In mid-2008, the corporate management changed. With the new management, the values and goals for the company changed. The company changed from being entrepreneurial to a centralized, command and control management system which contradicted my operating philosophy. I still continued to run the business in the way that I am describing here.
>
> In 2009, despite the sharp downturn, my team did uniquely well, exceeding budget and increasing ROI. Nevertheless, I was asked to resign. It does not matter whether or not my consistent values and goals were "right." My operating philosophy was now different from the values and the long-term direction the company was going. Thus, it was the right decision to ask me to resign as I was not in alignment on the values and goals.

<u>Align the Rest of the Team</u>

The second step is to ensure that all other employees support the values and goals of the business. For those below the leadership level, this is a slightly iterative process as you communicate the values and goals and begin to see who does and who does not support it. Shared values and attitude are essential. Do not slide on this one.

Enforce Accountability

As I will discuss in more detail in Chapter 18, you also need to let go of the "C" and "D" employees that have not performed and do not achieve their goals. Most of these employees may have been around for a while and are really nice, but most of their co-workers would agree that they should have been let go years before. Top management needs to be held equally accountable. In terms of turnarounds or under performing units, I have found that the "lead elephants" always need to be let go first. This should not be surprising because they were the ones who got the business into trouble in the first place, and they are the ones who would be most resistant to change.

Consider the DNA of the Business

Do you have people with the mentality and skill set that you will need to achieve the goals? If not, you will need to trade players to get people with the correct DNA to improve the gene pool of the company and make it fitter and able to thrive. I have seen this problem at many of the companies that I have been advising. In such cases, the businesses came of age and prospered in the boom years in mid-decade and have a strong DNA geared towards operations and fulfilling orders efficiently. In today's slower growth era, the successful companies will retain strong operational chops, but have a strong component of sales and business development to re-kindle growth. If that is not in a company's gene pool, then it must be brought into the company.

Don't Underestimate the Talent and Adaptability of Your Good Employees

Good employees can survive and even flourish in different roles and under different conditions. For the best, such change can be growth opportunities that round out their experiences and enable them to advance in the company. In turnarounds that I helped lead, we had a salesman and an engineer each become excellent and successful operations managers. Who would have thunk it?

Don't Forget Your Core Values

In relentlessly seeking alignment with the right people doing the right jobs, it is vital that the lay-offs, re-organizations, and terminations be done according to the values that you are espousing. I offer an anecdote from one of the companies we turned around.

> After the first few weeks of rolling out the plan, one of the top managers came to give his resignation. He did not have another job at the time. But, he realized that he just did not have what it would take to work in a business environment where you are being held accountable to perform. We had two options:
>
> 1. We could accept his resignation and save ourselves severance and other costs.
>
> 2. We could thank him for his honesty. We could then lay him off with the severance package we were offering all employees at that time. And we could allow him to collect unemployment.
>
> What did we do? In keeping with the core value of Winning Teamwork, we chose the second option. Even in the midst of a turnaround and lay-offs, you need to do the right thing for the people on your team. And you need to be seen doing the right thing for all your employees.

Translate the Business Goals into Three Specific Goals for Each Employee

A fundamental sales concept is that every customer is only tuned into radio station WII-FM – "What's In it For Me." Likewise, employees will see or read about the overall business goals. But, they may not understand the goals or see how these goals are relevant to what they do in their jobs on a day to day basis. As such, most employees quickly forget the business goals, thus reducing the employee's alignment to the goals and their engagement with the company.

You and your leadership team need to translate the overall business goals into specific and actionable goals for each unit of the business, each sub-unit, each man-

> *Napoleon once said that orders need to be so simple that they cannot be misunderstood. Likewise, for each employee their personal goals and how these goals fit into the overall business goals needs to be crystal-clear and kept front of mind.*

ager, and each employee. You need to cascade your goals down into these other specific, individualized goals.

Huh?!?

Let's try an example:

The overall business goals are:

1. Best in Class Customer Service and Responsiveness with Current Customers.

2. Increased Market Share and Penetration to New and Complementary Market Space.

3. Continued Refinement of High Volume Production while Enhancing Capability for Specialized and Customized Production.

With your 1 – 2 page "playbook" for each of these goals, you will set specific goals for each part of the business: the sales team, the customer service organization, project management, the marketing team, production, purchasing, engineering, finance and even information technology.

The production manager may have as goals:

1. Continue focus on fundamentals of safety, quality, efficiency, housekeeping and preventive maintenance.

2. Hire or train someone as an industrial engineer to focus on eliminating constraints and streamlining high volume production.

3. Set up separate area of facility and develop a leader to focus on low volume, specialized work.

Information technology may have goals as follows:

1. Continue focus on providing timely and accurate data to all internal and external stakeholders.

2. Work with finance and sales to institute metrics and provide data to measure customer service and responsiveness.

3. Work with production and finance to determine proper metrics and data required to measure efficiency and costs of production on low volume, specialized work.

By cascading down these goals to these levels, everyone in the organization will know what is in it for them. They will understand how what they do contributes to achieving the overall goals of the business.

Explain the Goals... Teach the Values

How do you ensure that the values that you espouse and your business goals are truly understood and shared by all employees throughout the organization? Your values and goals need to stick; they need to be front of mind; and they

> *"If you want to out-execute your competitors, you must communicate clear strategies and values, reinforce those values in everything the company does, and allow people the freedom to act, trusting and verifying that they will execute consistent with the values."*
>
> **Lou Gerstner**

need to be thought of on a daily basis.

Many companies will hang posters or plaques throughout the office or factory listing the values and goals. Other companies will hand out pens or mouse pads listing the values and goals. Still others will make a list of the values and goals the default screen saver on everyone's computer. These can all be helpful in getting the values and goals to be thought of daily. But, they are not sufficient.

To ensure that your values permeate the organization and that the company goals are clearly understood, you, as the leader, need to spend the time to teach the values and goals directly to the employees in your company.

What?!?

Yes, teach. As a leader, stand in front of groups, large and small, and directly explain, teach and preach your values and the company goals, how they were derived, and why they are important.

What to Teach?

The goal is to teach all members of your team about the company, about your values, and about the business goals. As Division President, I conducted countless teaching sessions, formally in a 2½ day class that I called "Precast University" and informally in small group settings. The purpose of these sessions was to ensure that everyone understood what the company did and to explain the values in the company and the goals that the leadership team had for the company.

First, I would give an overview of the company. I had a "show and tell" about the size and extent, the culture, the customers, and the products and services in the company. I was always shocked to discover how little people who had worked at the company knew about the company. Finance and human resources people would not know the products that we produced. Even production people would have no idea how our products and services were used or who our customers were.

After this introduction, I would explain the values that I wanted infused throughout the company. Then, I would lay out the business goals. I would explain the critical issues and opportunities facing the business and why we are doing what we are doing. Finally, I would explain how the overall goals cascaded down to each of them, and thus how each of their individual work contributed to realizing the overall goals of the company.

When and to Whom to Teach?

In addition to these Precast University sessions, I would review the values and business goals with the Vice Presidents and General Managers at formal General Manager Meetings. I would teach to up and coming managers at small group "Manager of Manager" forums. I would teach the values and goals as an introduction before other more specific (sales, production, negotiation, etc.) training sessions that I or others might be doing. Finally, when visiting plants or different departments, I would discuss the values and goals in informal small group "Lunch and Learn" sessions. The opportunities for teaching are endless. What is essential is to ensure that as many people as possible hear your message, both managers and employees.

You will need to conduct training sessions with your direct reports present and training sessions without your direct reports present. When your direct reports and their direct reports are in the same class at the same time, they are all hearing the same message. This reduces mis-communication and the lower level employees can be a check on whether their supervisors are following what you want them to do. When your direct reports are not present, employees are much more open and the interaction is livelier.

Why Teach Your Values and the Company Goals?
• *Helps Spread and Refine Your Message*
As leaders, we continue to over-estimate the penetration of messages to all levels of the organization. We may have been preaching a message for years and feel that we have communicated it to everyone possible, yet it still may not have penetrated down to the frontline. President Richard Nixon had it right when he wrote:

> About the time that you are writing a line you have written so often that
> you want to throw up, that is the time the American people will hear it.

By taking the time to teach your message directly and personally to the people throughout your organization, you get the opportunity to ensure that the company values and goals are heard directly and in person. In larger companies, this may be the only personal interaction that an employee will have with "the big boss". If that is the case, would it not be important that that interaction revolves around what you as a leader stand for and your goals for the business?

Surprisingly, the constant teaching and communication of your values and the company goals will have another benefit. It helps improve the message. When I do all this teaching, the general content of what I communicate rarely changes, but the words and how I communicate the message does change. Especially at the beginning, I might be stressing a point and see by the reaction in the group that I have lost them completely, either from confusion or (yes, I will admit it) sheer boredom. In the end, the message gets shorter and more relevant, with more examples and stories. It becomes "stickier" and is more likely to be understood and retained.

- *Forces You to Live the Values and Focus on the Business Goals*

Through teaching your values and communicating the business goals, you will be (over time) in front of hundreds of employees in large groups and small settings. You are on stage and the employees will directly see how well you live the values and focus on the business goals through your actions during the different sessions. Moreover, by teaching you will really understand the subject. The values and business goals will remain in the front of your mind. Each time that you teach, that little voice inside your head will be telling you how well or how poorly you are living up to your values and properly focusing on the goals. This will reduce the hypocrisy which cripples companies where leaders say one thing and do another. Done well, you will thus be able to lead by your visible example.

- *Develops Relationships with Employees Below the Level of Your Direct Reports*

By spending time directly with employees at all levels in both small and large groups, you will get to know many of them and connect with them on a personal level. You will get to know their names. You will get to know one or two things about them. In their body language, their engagement with you, and their questions and comments, you will learn a little about their personality and their style. In turn, they will learn about you. In short, you will begin to develop a relationship with them.

As discussed above, this occurs especially in those meetings where your direct reports (their supervisors) are not present. Through this budding relationship you will begin to know better what is going on in the frontline and with customers without the insulation of several layers of management. As discussed in Chapter 8, these relationships with employees layers down in your organization will help you to know how your managers are managing and to understand the level of alignment in the organization.

Countless surveys expose some dirty little secrets of business today. Most employees in most companies...

- Do not know the values of their company and what their company stands for.
- Do not know the business goals and how these goals translate into what they do on a daily basis.
- Have little interaction with any leaders in their company outside of their direct supervisor.

By teaching your values, explaining the business goals, and interacting directly with employees throughout your company, you, as a leader, can dramatically improve the alignment of your employees with your values and goals and increase the engagement and motivation employees feel in their daily work lives. With improved alignment (everyone rowing in the same direction) and increased engagement and motivation (everyone dedicated and committed to rowing harder to win the race), you will be developing the "Winning Teamwork" essential for long-term business success.

SECTION IV – WINNING TEAMWORK

CHAPTER 15 –
WINNING TEAMWORK

"The achievements of an organization are the results
of the combined effort of each individual."

Vince Lombardi

For those readers who are about to undertake their first position
with full profit and loss (P&L) authority, welcome to the club. Within
a few months, you will understand what the grizzled veterans with
P&L experience already know: "it is all about the people."

All leaders spend significant time and energy on people issues.
Some people issues can be delegated to the human resources staff,
but not all. And certainly not the ones involving direct reports or
high level managers.

Just to give you a taste of what to expect, here are some of the
issues that I have dealt with involving just direct reports or senior
managers in my companies over ten years' time:

- Employee theft
- Lying
- Accounting and other fraud
- Failed drug tests by 20+ year veterans
- Blatant favoritism and nepotism
- Affairs between supervisors and direct reports

Yet, I have been fortunate. Under my leadership, no one in any of my companies has ever been critically injured or killed. Knock on wood. And my business has been successful, profitable, growing and continually exceeding budget and other goals.

As a leader, leading people and building a team is always challenging. It can also be frustrating and even sad. You will see good people whom you have gotten to know and care for, do stupid things that can destroy their careers and even their personal lives.

And yet, leading people and building a team is the most exciting, satisfying and even joyful part of being a leader. You will see your good employees do extraordinary things. And together, despite long odds, you will experience the tremendous satisfaction of winning as a team.

Creating Winning Teamwork is essential in building a successful business.

Several years ago, I asked eight of my veteran General Managers to each give two pieces of advice to a new General Manager about what he needed to learn and do as he settled into his position. Out of the sixteen pieces of advice, eleven of them related to people and leading the team.

1.   Learn to hire people

2.   Learn to fire people

3.   Pay attention to people on the front lines of the business

4.   Ask people: "What has gone wrong today?" and "What has gone right today?"

5.   Surround yourself with good people

6.   Catch someone doing something right every day

7. Learn how to delegate to your team

8. Treat everyone fairly

9. Listen

10. Keep your door open

11. Have empathy

Obviously, this is a less than scientific survey, but it makes the point. People management and building a winning team is a critically important fundamental, a pre-requisite to having a successful business.

Yet, of all aspects of leadership, actually leading people is the most challenging to teach and coach. So much revolves around having the experience of doing it.   As George Bernard Shaw said:

> Experience is not something one can pass to another. For this, you have to go through the fires.

Notwithstanding this challenge, my objective in Section IV is to give insight and guidance to help you develop an effective and winning team.

To build your Winning Team that executes, you need:
- Communication
- Accountability
- Motivation and Engagement
- Recognition
- Continual Learning

CHAPTER 16 –
CONSISTENT EXECUTION

"The difference between a company and its competitors is its ability to execute; this is the critical difference for success."

Larry Bossidy and Ram Charan

- *Daily Execution*
- *Speedy*
- *Decisive*

The over-riding objective of this book is to help you and your business win. Doing the Right Thing, Winning Teamwork, and Customer Service all help move your business forward and enable it to succeed. But, having the right strategies in place with the right motivated talent in the right market niche – all this means nothing if your team cannot consistently execute, achieve its goals, and win in the marketplace.

The three keys for consistent execution are as follows:
- Daily Execution
- Speed
- Decisiveness

Daily Execution

The daily grind of both you and your team living the values and executing on the business goals determines whether a company will succeed or not. In his 2005 statement in the Berkshire Hathaway Annual Report, Warren Buffett summed up well the utmost importance of executing daily.

> Every day, in countless ways, the competitive position of each of our businesses grows either weaker or stronger. If we are delighting customers, eliminating unnecessary costs, and improving our products and services, we gain strength. But, if we treat customers with indifference or tolerate bloat, our businesses will wither. On a daily basis, the effects of our actions are imperceptible; cumulatively, though, their consequences are enormous. When our long-term competitive position improves as a result of these unnoticeable actions, we describe the phenomenon as "widening the moat." And doing that is essential if we are to have the kind of business we want a decade or two from now. We always, of course, hope to earn more money in the short-term.

> But, when short-term and long-term conflict, widening the moat must take precedence. If a management makes bad decisions in order to hit short-term earnings targets, and consequently gets behind the eight ball in terms of costs, customer satisfaction or brand strength, no amount of subsequent brilliance will overcome the damage that has been inflicted. Take a look at the dilemmas of managers in the auto and airline industries today as they struggle with the huge problems handed them by their predecessors. Charlie Munger [Warren Buffett's Number Two] is fond of quoting Ben Franklin's "An ounce of prevention is worth a pound of cure." But sometimes no amount of cure will overcome the mistakes of the past.

Execution requires daily and relentless focus and prioritization on your most important issues. This applies to both the individual employee and to the company as a whole.

Many employees and organizations live in the here and now. That means that they are focused on what is immediately in front of them that needs to be done. In doing this, they will usually dedicate sufficient time to activities that are both urgent and important. They will also spend a disproportionate amount of time and attention on urgent but non-important tasks. The challenge is to combat this focus on the non-important urgent in order to spend sufficient time and attention on the tasks that are not urgent but important.

To fight this "tyranny of the urgent" requires daily reinforcement and focus on the most important issue. In the military, the most important is defined as the Commander's Intent. The Commander's Intent represents the one thing that if accomplished will make the day a successful day.

To apply in business, review and write down the daily Commander's Intent at both the beginning and end of every day.

- <u>Beginning of the Day</u>: "The one thing that I will accomplish today to make this day a success is…."
- <u>End of the Day</u>: "Did I accomplish that one thing?" and "What will be the one thing that I need to accomplish tomorrow to make tomorrow a success?"

Further, you and your employees need to ask yourself literally dozens of times a day on small, medium and large issues: What is Most Important? Then, get that most important done.

> *"Get the important done first. What's been on your to-do list the longest? Start it first thing in the morning, don't check E-Mail and don't allow interruptions or lunch until you finish."*
>
> **Timothy Ferriss**

In addition, to execute daily it is important to avoid distractions and to avoid slipping into "comfort" mode.

Avoid Distractions

In business today, the opportunity for distraction is endless. This includes all the distractions of the urgent but unimportant that range from meetings to E-Mail to Internet surfing. Due to these distractions and constant interruptions, employees and companies often do not have solid block of times to get finished what needs to be finished. Interruptions are particularly pernicious as there is an inescapable setup time for all tasks before you are getting back into full swing.

> A "can I have one moment?" interruption will usually last ten to fifteen minutes. After that, inevitably comes a quick check of the E-Mail and then another ten minutes to get back to working solidly on what you were doing before the interruption. In short, that "just one minute" interruption took up thirty minutes. For someone making $100,000 that one minute cost about $25!

- *Reduce the Transition Times*

Of course, you cannot avoid all distractions. But, when distracted or interrupted, a best practice would be to get back to work as soon as possible. Work on transitioning quickly without taking breaks or taking quick checks of E-Mail. In the above case, with a focus on the transition and not checking the E-Mail, perhaps, the person could have been back to work in only twelve minutes reducing the cost of the interruption to only $10. Transitioning quickly also helps prevent procrastination from creeping in.

- *Batch Your Work*

Create one hour blocks of quiet times (allowing for interruptions in the case of true emergencies), where the E-Mail system is shut down, the phone is turned off, and you are dedicated to the most important tasks. On a company level, attack the most important action item in one fell swoop and get it fully and completely done. Create time blocks where the routine, unimportant yet necessary tasks can be completed. Ideally, these would be at times when your concentration is weakest; usually, right before lunch or at the end of the day.

- *Define Fewer Things as Urgent*

With fewer urgent items, you can often reduce five "quick one minute" calls to one call about all five issues. It is important to realize that what is urgent for you may not be urgent for the business as a whole.

- *Consciously Ignore*

Individual employees and companies need to consciously make the effort to ignore much of the information and stimulation in the environment. Not every tidbit of information and everything that you are curious about needs your attention.

- *Learn to Say "No"*

Master the art of refusal and learn to say "No." Darren Hardy, the publisher of *Success* magazine, offers a story about Richard Branson and his ability to say "No" in order to focus on the important.

> A while back, after our *Success* cover feature with the knighted Sir Richard Branson, we had a client contact us to inquire about hiring Richard Branson to speak at their conference. So, we had someone inquire and Sir Richard declined. The client then offered $250,000 for an hour talk; Sir Richard declined. They then raised it to $500,000. Sir Richard declined. Then we asked how much it WOULD take to get Sir Richard to attend. The response from his people was, "no amount of money would matter." They said, "Right now Richard has three main priorities he is focused on and he will only allocate his time to those three priorities, and speaking for a fee is not one of them."

Avoid Being a "Comfort Junkie"

Both individuals and companies are often "comfort junkies." They avoid doing tasks that they do not like to do or that make them feel uncomfortable.

> I have certainly been guilty of this when I have delayed confronting an awkward employee situation such as a non-performing employee or the employee that committed fraud as discussed in Chapter 10. It

is not that I did not know that I needed to act. It just made me uncomfortable, so I procrastinated and did not get it done punctually.

Yet, one element of Doing the Right Thing is that we are not paid to do what we like to do. Rather, we are paid to do what must be done. To execute and achieve the goals requires unparalleled focus on the most important tasks or

> *"What we fear doing most is usually what we most need to do."*
>
> **Timothy Ferriss**

issues whether or not we are comfortable doing them or whether or not we like to do them.

Speedy

In successfully executing goals, speed matters.
- The quicker that you complete a task, the sooner you can get on to the next task.
- The quicker that you respond back to a customer, the more likely you are to win their trust and possibly their business.

So, how can you speed up what gets done?

Get to the Point

Get started on things immediately. Don't waste time even considering procrastinating. Once something is started, move on it. In conversations and work, get to the point cutting down on chit chat and get right to business.

One of my Vice-Presidents of Sales and Marketing was exceptional at this. We might have a meeting and decide on a course of action. Literally, before I could step out the door of his office, he was on the phone beginning the task. One time, we had a 6:00 pm meeting, and I asked him to follow up on a difficult issue that I would need an answer for in a day and a half. The next morning, I was flying out early on business. When I landed at 8:30 am, he had already left a message on my phone with the answer. I asked how he had done this so quickly and he recited the names of the eleven people to whom he had spoken that morning to get the answer. Arriving back in town, I looked at his call log. He had made more than eighteen calls in that short few hours, but had only been able to actually speak with eleven people.

To facilitate getting to the point, ensure that you understand the nature of the problem or issue. I have often seen people procrastinate because a task appears to be difficult. Only when they had completed the task did they realize

> *"The wise man does at once what the fool does finally."*
>
> *Niccolo Machiavelli*

how quick and easy it was. So, skim through the report, the presentation, or the work assignment and then determine how long it will take to get done. Then, either get it done immediately or set up a block of time to get it done in one fell swoop.

Finally, getting to the point creates a sense of urgency in all that you do. With this urgency comes momentum and the expectation that you will work more quickly and more ruthlessly to get things done.

Keep Short Deadlines

Not everything is perfect in business. I have alluded to this before when speaking about the 80 / 20 rule or about the 80 / 100 rule. It is often true that to complete a task or respond back to someone at a 90% correct level may take only a few minutes, whereas to respond back at a 98% - 100% correct level may take 5 days. Err on the side of the few minute answer.

To get things done within the few minutes, I would create short deadlines. As such, the employees were forced to prioritize and focus on only the most important issues. Further, to assist them in keeping short deadlines, I would often reduce the task. For example, if we had a meeting, I would ask that the meeting notes be completed by the end of the day and require that they be at most one page. This is a double win: the task is completed punctually and the notes focus only on the essential.

Likewise, keep short deadlines on meetings and stick to those deadlines. Wal-Mart CEO Mike Duke is known for walking out of meetings at the end time even in the middle of a discussion. By sticking to and respecting these short meeting times, it ensures that the next meeting will be more productive especially at the outset when many meetings often get bogged down and off track.

It is good to remember the words of General George Patton:

> Perfection is the enemy of the good. By this, I mean that a good plan executed with great vigor now is better than a perfect plan next week. Success is a very simple thing; and the determining characteristics are confidence, speed and audacity — none of which can ever be perfect, but they can be good.

Think Critical Path

Thinking of the critical path helps to speed all activities along. Critical path is a project management technique that looks at the time element for each required step to complete a goal. It then strives to shorten the time to accomplish a goal by performing the steps as rapidly as possible and in parallel.

> In the discussion on finding root cause in Chapter 13, I gave an example where not entering sales orders delayed the purchasing of a long-lead time item which then delayed the product delivery. In this case, the key element in getting things done quickly was to realize what was on the critical path. You could perform all the other tasks with great rapidity, but if you had to wait on the long-lead time item, the project would be delayed.

To execute rapidly requires that the employees and you as a leader realize what is on the critical path and focus to get those items done as quickly as possible even if some things need to be done out of turn or less efficiently. To determine the critical path, map out the process and find out where the path can be shortened.

Critical path and process mapping are most often used in operations, especially when trying to introduce lean production techniques. Process mapping (also known as value mapping) charts the process and looks at how much time is actually spent working on the product or activity. It is usually eye-opening; products that might take two days to enter and leave production may only be worked on for 45 minutes during that time. By looking at the critical path and shortening the delays along the path, products and processes can be completed significantly quicker. This can be applied throughout business.

> When I was performing financial analysis in the early 1990's, the average time to complete and disseminate the month-end reports was 28 days. By focusing on the critical path and corralling some senior managers for their analysis or approval, I was able to reduce it to 4 days. This was still not "world-class", but was a significant improvement that allowed the operating executives to get information that was much fresher and more relevant.

In mastering critical path, it is necessary for management to avoid being the roadblocks. In the example above, top management was the roadblock as reports would sit on their desks for days at a time awaiting their analysis or final approval. Yes, these leaders had many things on their plate and may have been out traveling. Nevertheless, their lack of punctual response delayed the reports making them, if truth be told, nearly useless. It is for this reason that I believe so strongly in the importance of leaders' returning phone calls, responding promptly to E-Mails, and being decisive. A delayed response or approval inevitably delays the whole project or task.

Finally, we each need to realize that our own individual effectiveness and priorities are subordinate to the overall business effectiveness and priorities. We may have to do a task more

> *"The secret to success lies in careful preparation followed by speedy and decisive execution."*
>
> **Napoleon**

inefficiently or earlier in the process than we want in order to ensure that the overall goal is achieved as quickly as possible.

Decisiveness

To have a business execute consistently, individual employees need to be given the authority and the support to act quickly and decisively. In countless academic studies, this idea of rapid and decisive action differentiates the fast-moving entrepreneurial company from the slow-moving bureaucratic companies.

You create or re-create a culture of decisive action by making decisions at lower levels, allowing for failure, and being decisive in the decisions you make.

Make Decisions at Lower Levels

The goal is to make all decisions at the lowest possible level where the person making the decision has accountability for the results of the decision. In nearly all cases, this would be a lower

> *"It is wonderful how someone's abilities and commitment sky-rocket when you give them the responsibility and accountability to do what they can do."*

level than many decisions are currently made. The lower the decision level the more rapidly the decision can be made, the more accountability that the person making the decision has for the decision, and the more training and growth that that person receives.

I would often get a phone call from one of my General Managers asking me to be a sounding board as they struggled to make a difficult decision. Together, we would go over the issues surrounding the decision, the different options, and the decision that the General Manager was considering. After doing this, the General Manager would often ask me what I thought of their decision. I would usually respond with: "I do not disagree." This answer meant that it was their decision to make and their decision alone. Even though I was not saying whether I agreed or disagreed with their course of action, I was telling them that what they had decided was not off the wall crazy. Occasionally, this answer would be infuriating for the General Manager because the purpose of the call was really for me to be a crutch or a security blanket. And I was refusing to be that for them. It was their decision to make and their accountability to answer for that decision.

In many organizations, no one in the organization is allowed to make a decision without the boss's approval. As such, everything revolves around the boss' schedule and priorities and execution lags; the boss is truly a "roadblock." These organizations inevitably

> *"Recently, I was asked if I was going to fire an employee who made a mistake that cost the company $600,000. 'No, I replied, I just spent $600,000 training him.'"*
>
> **Thomas J. Watson, founder of IBM**

fail to execute. First, employees have no ownership in the decisions that are made. Second, employees are under-utilized. Without empowering good employees to make decision for which they are being held accountable, the organization is not taking advantage of all their talents and experiences.

Allow for Failure

Many companies allow their employees to take actions or make decisions, but they do not allow them to fail. In the employee's mind, decision making becomes a one-way bet:

> Make the decision correctly, you keep your job. Make a wrong decision, you lose your job.

For the employees, it does not pay to take any risk or action if the consequences are so extreme. They will just keep their heads down and do what they are told. More than anything, it is this failure to take initiative and make decisions that leads to rampant bureaucracy.

To realize decisiveness in your business, you need to have employees be allowed to make and learn from mistakes.

> In the first 14 of my 16 years at Oldcastle, we had a standing expression that it was better to seek forgiveness than to ask for permission. What this allowed us to do was to respond rapidly to changing circumstances and quickly seize opportunities as soon as they presented themselves to us. Moreover, it gave the General Managers who were running their businesses a strong identity of themselves as entrepreneurs accountable for the success of their companies. Of course, we made a number of mistakes. But, the successes from our rapid and decisive actions clearly out-weighed the failures.

Warren Buffett (once again) summarizes well the importance of allowing mistakes in order to have decisive action:

> We would rather suffer the visible costs of a few bad decisions than incur the many invisible costs that come from decisions made too slowly-or not at all-because of a stifling bureaucracy.

> *"Any commander who fails to exceed his authority is not of much use to his subordinates."*
>
> *Admiral Arleigh Burke*

Be Decisive in your Actions

As the leader, you need to lead by example in being decisive. This does not mean foolhardily plunging off of cliffs. Rather, it requires that you take intelligent and decisive action, make most decisions quickly, be opportunistic when needed, and admit and even celebrate the mistakes that you make.

> Decisiveness in decisions is vital. Make 80% of your decisions on the spot; 15% need to mature; 5% need not be made at all.[5]

In addition, be decisive in not making decisions. Resist the urge to make the decisions that your team should make.

> In the early years of leading my division, I would be making countless decisions. Of course, I was "making it happen" and pushing hard to improve the business. But, I was making so many decisions that when the weekend came, I did not care what my family and I did just as long as I did not decide what we were to do. I did not want to make any decisions about anything. After a while, I realized that I was just making too many of the decisions for the business. I needed to push decision-making down to lower levels even when others wanted me to make the decision.

In short, if you have a case of "decision exhaustion", then take a cold, hard look at the decisions that you are making. Most likely, it is time to get your employees to make the decisions that they need to make. Thus, you remove yourself as a bottleneck, empower your team, and make them accountable to execute daily, speedily, and decisively.

CHAPTER 17 – COMMUNICATION

> "The greatest problem with communication
> is the illusion that it is done."
>
> George Bernard Shaw

- *What is Effective Communication?*
- *How to Communicate Effectively?*
- *Listening*

What is Effective Communication?

"But, I was never told!

"But, you did not tell me that it was that important."

"That is not how I understood what you told me."

In a business, communication takes place all the time. As business leaders, we are confident that...

- We told them the task
- We told them how important the task was
- They understood exactly what we said

We thus proceed forward certain that the communication has taken place. Only to realize later that the communication had not taken place as we thought; it was only an illusion that there had been communication. The crux of leadership communication is to bridge this chasm between what the leader says and what the people do.

In my Precast University class on communication, I would begin with a question.

> If a tree falls in the forest and no one is around to hear it, does it make a sound?

The answer is that it does not make a sound, it makes sound waves. Not until someone (or something) is around to hear it do the sound waves get turned into a sound. Likewise, in communication, if you are talking and your audience does not understand what you have said, you are not communicating. You are just uttering words (and creating sound waves).

So what is effective communication?

Effective communication means achieving a complete, mutual understanding (not necessarily agreement) between parties.

- Complete - all the facts (who, what, where, when, how, why) and the relative priorities.
- Mutual - all parties have the same understanding

Or as Vince Lombardi has said:

> Communication doesn't take place until your people: hear or see what you say; understand it; believe it; believe you mean it; remember it; internalize it; and begin to use it themselves.

Unfortunately, there are numerous barriers and filters that make effective communication difficult:

- **Our skill level in communicating.** How clearly do we communicate? Does the listener understand all the terms and the context of everything that we have said? Do we keep things short and simple and thus able to be understood and retained?

- **The distractions of our relationship, environment and culture.** As the business leader, do we intimidate the other person and make it less likely that they will speak up or say that they do not understand? Does the culture of the other person make it a loss of face to say that he does not know or understand? Does the situation make it less likely that the communication will be effective?
- **The listener's learning style.** How does the listener best understand and remember? By reading? Visually? By doing?
- **The listener's listening skills.** Does the listener pay attention and listen well?

As a result of all these challenges, most communication is only 30% effective. But, to build an aligned and winning team, the values, direction and goals must be communicated effectively to each individual.

> *"I speak and speak, but the listener retains only the words he is expecting."*
>
> **Marco Polo**

How to Communicate Effectively?

Keep Your Message Simple (KISS) – Less is More!

The average person can remember at most three to five items at a time. Communicating any more than that will ensure incomplete and ineffective communication. As such, the burden is on the speaker to put significant thought into the three to five points that he is trying to convey and to organize these thoughts in a succinct and well-organized way. As discussed previously, be specific, and use terms and language that the other person will understand.

During my Precast University training sessions, I would create teams of four and do a "communication relay" (similar to the child's game of telephone) to see how effectively and accurately a message could be communicated from team member to team member. In having seen this in action more than 100 times, no team every got it right the first time. First, the person speaking would always insist on communicating non-essential information. In every case, the more excess information that people tried to communicate the less the key points were understood and passed along. Second, employees used terms and concepts that they understood, and they would assume that the listener understood these terms and concepts as well.

As an example, I had an excellent employee who was Ukrainian and only spoke fair English. In his communication relay, I included a message that contained the name of Andriy Shevchenko, a well-known Ukrainian soccer player. I then teamed this employee up with another employee who was a soccer fanatic and two others. The communication of the name went flawlessly between the Ukrainian and the soccer fanatic, but the other two absolutely butchered the name and so the message was lost. Interestingly, despite the obvious difficulty neither the Ukrainian employee nor the soccer fanatic explained the name and neither of the other two employees asked for clarification on the name. The lesson learned was clear; you cannot assume that your listener understands all the terms that you use.

Whenever possible, the best forum for communication is one-to-one. In a group format, the message gets diffused and it is difficult for the speaker to pick up on visual clues of understanding or lack of understanding. Further, in a group setting, the listener is unlikely to ask for any kind of clarification or correction.

As the speaker, remember that it is not important what you say...only what they hear and understand. To ensure that communication is taking place, it is your responsibility to understand their listening styles and

> *"If only I could never open my mouth until the abstract idea had reached its highest point — and had become a story!"*
>
> *Zorba the Greek*

even their method of learning (do they prefer to hear it, read it, see a picture, or see it demonstrated?).

Finally, in communicating the three points, consider telling stories as they resonate. They are better understood and better remembered.

Practice the Rule of Ten

A new concept or idea may need to be communicated as many as ten times before being internalized by the audience. As discussed in the Chapter on achieving alignment, leaders should promote daily, weekly, monthly communication. This includes communicating the values and the goals of the business and the expectations for each individual. In doing this, consistently communicate the progress towards the goals: how far the individual or team has come and the remaining gap between the current reality and the goal.

The regular communication of the Rule of Ten is vital. First, it helps ensure that the team believes that you mean it. Many employees are accustomed to the pigeon manager who screams and yells about one point, but then forgets about it and never mentions it again. As such, employees are conditioned to assume that a message that is not communicated consistently is not really that important and can be ignored. Second, through this communication, you keep the team in the know, filling a void that could otherwise become occupied by rumor and innuendos. Finally, to effectively use the Rule of Ten, all but requires that your keep your message simple and limited to three to five points.

Make Clarifying and Confirming a Habit

To ensure complete and mutual understanding require that the other person to whom you are communicating summarizes the major points of the discussion. In many cases, the listener will not have understood the points. But, unless you follow up directly, they will generally not ask for clarification. This is especially true in cultures where any sign of weakness can be considered a loss of face and where there may be language difficulties.

One summer, my family and I went to Club Med in the South of France. There, I took tennis lessons. Of course, everything was in French. Although I can speak passable French, I am by no means fluent. During the tennis class, the teacher would explain a point and then detail the next exercise. At the end, he would finish by asking me: "Comprenez Vous, David? [Do you understand]." I always quickly responded: "Oui [Yes]". I did not want the rest of the class to know that I really did not understand what the instructor was saying. Of course, I always botched the following exercise, twice hitting one of the other players with the ball while they were looking the other way. After a few times, a very polite and bi-lingual fellow student began translating for me.

This story highlights two points. First, even though I am not timid, I did not ask for clarification because I did not want to look stupid. Second, clarifying and confirming is more than just the simple question of: "Do you understand?" You need to probe to ensure that they understood and can put into their own words what you were communicating.

Some suggestions on clarifying and communicating in daily business:

1. **Summarize.** In one-to-one communication, have the person to whom you are communicating summarize the major ideas of a discussion. You will need to be directive in confirming with them what is to be done, by when, the relative priority and what results are to be achieved. But, you will likely not be directive as to how it gets done.

2. **Document in Writing.** After summarizing, follow-up with a written summary of the communication. For meetings, write up meeting notes with specific assignments and deadlines and immediately distribute.

3. **Follow Up.** Plan and document the follow up… and then to do it.

Listening

In Chapter 12, I discussed listening in some detail. As such, I have only a few points to add here.

First, listening to your team is absolutely crucial in getting the best ideas to come forward. Without listening you are not taking advantage of everything that your well-compensated employees have to offer. I like the quote from Larry King:

> I remind myself every morning: nothing that I say this day will teach me anything. So, if I am going to learn, I must do it by listening.

Second, I have a quick quiz.

<u>Quiz</u>: Check any of the boxes that may apply to you or someone you know:

- ☐ To prevent getting too bored, I multi-task while listening and work on other things (type on the computer, surf the Internet, text)
- ☐ Since I already know what the other person will say, I just tune out
- ☐ While listening, I think about what I am going to say next rather than listen to what the other person is saying.
- ☐ I usually interrupt when the other person starts to slow down, says something I don't agree with, or when I just get too tired of hearing what he has to say.
- ☐ When I am tuning out, I repeat a throwaway response (e.g. right, yes, "I understand," uh-huh) to make him think that I am paying attention.

Most likely, each of has checked at least one box. We are not perfect listeners and need to do better.

Third, I have a surprise. As leaders, we cannot and should not ever become textbook perfect listeners.

> Several years ago, I had just attended a leadership development class in which listening skills were taught. Coming back from the class, I decided that I would try to listen as perfectly as I could for a few days to see what would happen. Most importantly, I would wait until the other person had finished speaking, and I would not interrupt. I lasted all of two days.
>
> On day one, I had a meeting with one of my new product salespeople. Thirty excruciating minutes later, I had said exactly 8 words and had heard the same point three times and was bored to tears. On day two, I traveled to meet with a group for dinner and a few beers. During the beers, I got way-laid by a project manager who talked my ear off incessantly for 45 interminable minutes before I had to interrupt and use the bathroom excuse to win my freedom back.

In short, you cannot be the perfect listener, you will need to direct the conversation as your time is expensive. We can, however, be better listeners, even if it means being blunt listeners. This would include giving 100% attention and not interrupting in many cases. But, it would also include setting a deadline for the conversation up front; it would include interrupting on occasion to direct the conversation and keep the conversation on deadline. In short, set the ground rules for the conversation ahead of time and then follow them.

Even small changes in your listening skills with more attention being paid and one or two fewer interruptions will be noticed by the other person and be appreciated.

CHAPTER 18 – ACCOUNTABILITY

"To succeed as a team is to hold all of the members accountable for their expertise."

Mitchell Caplan (CEO, E*Trade)

- *Businesses lacking accountability*
- *Creating an accountable business*
- *The benefits of an accountable business*
- *How to over-manage accountability*

In a well-managed and well-led organization, a culture of accountability permeates the business. Each individual, each team, each profit center, each division is responsible for their success.

Businesses Lacking Accountability

It is easy to spot organizations where accountability is lacking.

Promises and Commitments Are Not Kept

Phone calls and E-Mails are not responded to. Deadlines are not kept. Endless meetings are endlessly long and end with nothing resolved and nothing committed to.

CYA (Cover Your A**), Blame and Finger Pointing are Pervasive

Common and accepted statements would include: "I did my part. But they did not." "It's not my job."

Excuses Abound

Examples would include statement such as: "Our company did not perform because of the economy, because of the weather, because of government regulation, because of…" "I did not make my sales numbers because our competitors are stupid and giving it away, because the market stinks, because our prices are too high, because I do not have enough resources, because…"

Non-Performance is Tolerated, Especially at the Senior Level

As an anecdote, in one company I have worked with, one senior leader had not made his numbers in 10 out of the last 11 years, but still continued in his role. In some companies, non-performers may even be promoted due to "having the right skill set," friendship, nepotism, etc.

Denial

"It is not my fault." Passing the buck. "But, I did not know what to do. I was never told."

Risk-Taking is Minimal

It is better and safer to be conventionally wrong than to be unconventionally right[6]. Inertia and inaction take over as everyone

---

6   From the economist John Maynard Keynes who wrote: "Worldly wisdom teaches that it is better for reputation to fail conventionally then to succeed unconventionally."

"waits and sees" what will happen next instead of taking the initiative to make things better.

Creating an Accountable Business

To have accountability in any business, the leader and his team must lead by example, master and use the management and leadership basics, and deal with non-performance.

<u>Lead by Your Example</u>
- *Accountability Starts at the Top*

   The business leader is accountable to build a better business and does not allow un-kept promises, CYA, denial and excuses for himself or for any of his leadership team. Senior leaders who do not perform are dealt with directly: they are not promoted; and they are not "kicked upstairs" to useless and bureaucratic staff positions.
- *Accountability Continues With the Individual Employee and Manager*

   Each individual does what he says. Each individual takes responsibility for successfully accomplishing his or her assigned tasks. Each individual takes ownership for his or her results. Employees are hired based on their ability, their track record, and their willingness to be accountable for their results.
- *This Accountability is Pervasive Throughout the Organization and Not Just on the Front Lines*

   Managers and staff people are as accountable as those in line positions. Many organizations have strict accountability on the front lines: production workers are measured on efficiency and quality daily; salespeople's sales quotas are assiduously tracked. But, this accountability trails off in other areas that are not as easily measured and where the results of the individual's actions are not as direct and immediate, such as with staff roles and management roles. The "accountable" organization ensures that everyone top to bottom is held accountable for his results.

Master and Use the Management and Leadership Basics

- *The Values of the Company and the Goals for Each Individual are Simple, Clear and Very Well-Communicated*

  To hold people accountable requires that they know and fully understand exactly what they are being held accountable for. Further, they need to understand how their goals fit in with the larger goals of the company. If their goals are crystal clear, front of mind, and understood to be important, then accountable employees are more likely to achieve the goals. And they would be more understanding of the consequences of not achieving them, both personally and for the health of the business.

- *Management Consistently Follows Up and Evaluates Employees' Progress Towards Their Goals*

  These fundamental management skills are pervasive and consistent over time. Constant follow-up ensures that everything is on track. Support and problem solving by management is used to provide assistance when issues arise. The goal is to do everything possible to help your employees realize their goals.

- *Each Employee is Respected as Being an Integral Part of a Winning Team*

  The accountability does not come at the expense of listening to and profiting from the insights of the employees. Feedback loops exist to ensure that the goals and objectives continue to make sense. If not, they are changed. New ideas and risk-taking are encouraged and are rewarded even if that means missing a previously agreed to metric. Further, the employees that are always accountable are thanked and recognized. These employees may do nothing heroic except do exactly what they are asked to do day in and day out. As such, they can often be forgotten and feel under appreciated.

Deal With Non-Performance

The tolerance of non-performance is probably the most pervasive issue in most companies, especially in senior ranks.

> In my career, I have not been afraid to fire direct reports, including General Managers. Nevertheless, I have to admit that I have struggled with this and terminated some people later than I should have and left non-performers in positions too long.

In theory, it is simple, hold people accountable, do everything that you can do to help them succeed. If they do not perform then either find a useful role for them (unlikely) or terminate them. In theory, it is simple. In practice, it is not so easy.

"When someone does not produce and does not improve, it is not fair to them to keep them on. They cannot possibly enjoy not being successful, and it is arrogant on our part to believe that they could not be successful doing something else."

The Leadership Machine

First, for well-run, lean companies, there is the reality, especially at senior levels, that there is nowhere to go but out. Most mid-sized and larger companies are growing too slowly to create many new and different senior level positions. Less well-run companies will shunt people into staff or bureaucratic positions, but this just creates more layers and blockage of the arteries for these companies.

> I have experience with a technology company that was once phenomenally successful. To avoid terminating non-performers, the company inserted them into newly created supervisory positions. At its flagship plant, the business operated with five layers of supervision between the Plant Manager and the 250 people actually building the product. On average, each supervisor had 2½ direct reports. The resulting arteriosclerosis from these additional layers hindered execution and diffused accountability so much that the business failed.

Second, there is familiarity and the humanity of the leader. You may have worked with the person in question for years. You may know his wife and children personally. He may have done great work several years ago that truly helped to advance your career. So you think, is this how I re-pay him?

Third, there is the challenge of the "Peter Principle". The Peter Principle suggests that people rise in organizations because they have been successful. They then stop rising when they have stopped being successful and reached "their level of incompetence." When someone is in such a role, you have a challenge. They are in a position where they are no longer successful. To improve the business they need to be moved out of that position. But where do they go? It is unlikely that there is another position at that same level where they can use their talents. And demotions rarely work out well.[7]

Fourth, there is often the feeling that there are no better alternatives to the "C" player that you currently have. There may be few internal candidates as many organizations have not developed a pipeline of up and coming leaders. Further, the external labor market remains terribly dysfunctional. Despite the overwhelming talent that is available most leaders feel that there are few good candidates, especially at the higher levels. This is inaccurate; but, few companies spend the continual time and effort trying to know about talent in the wider market. Since the perception is that no one else can do the job, the leader is resigned to being stuck with the marginal performer.

Because it is difficult and unpleasant, most companies continue to tolerate non-performance at all levels. But, dealing with non-performance is crucial to have accountability permeate your business. George Bradt, a specialist in leadership on-boarding, summarizes:

> The number one thing high performers want is for management to act
> on low performers so that the whole group can do better. Choosing

---

7   Demotions generally work only in situations where there is an opportunity for greater money in the new, subordinate position, e.g., demoting a sales manager to the position of a well-paid commission salesperson.

to act on people who are in the wrong roles now or will soon be in the wrong roles is generally not the most enjoyable part of leadership. But it is in an essential part.

Dealing with non-performance needs to be done quickly and decisively, yet compassionately.

In my own experience, I have at times acted too slowly. Overall, I have been involved in the termination of more than 20 senior managers or General Managers. I don't write this as a point of pride to communicate how tough I am. It is just the reality in business. In more than half of these cases, at least one (and sometimes many) respected employee have asked either the General Manager or me what took us so long. By our own inertia and not dealing with non-performers we had been unfair to the rest of the team.

In some companies that I have worked with, the leaders were benevolent and refused to deal with non-performance decisively for years. Instead, they waited until the recent sharp economic downturn and laid-off the non-performers in a wave of re-structuring. From the perspective of the laid-off employee, the leaders were far from compassionate. These employees were laid off at a time when the economy was at its worst with new job opportunities scarce. This often caused these employees economic hardships that they may not have had if they had been laid-off earlier and found a more suitable position in that better economic climate.

Finally, handle a termination for non-performance, as with any employee separation, correctly and with dignity.

- The employee needs to understand exactly what is required of him.
- The employee needs to be given the resources and the management follow-up, support and problem solving assistance.

- The company's discipline process needs to be followed. For companies without a discipline policy, this would require a formal oral warning and a formal and blunt written warning that spells out that the alternative to not achieving the goals is termination.
- The actual termination needs to be handled with grace.

I would tell my managers that when you fire someone for non-performance you should be able to sleep well the night before, secure in the knowledge that you had done everything possible to communicate and work out the performance issues. It should be clear that the non-performer had, in fact, really fired himself.

The Benefits of an Accountable Organization

<u>The Organization is Fairer and More of a Meritocracy</u>

Since performance is required and non-performance has consequences, there is less chance for favoritism, nepotism and other morale-sapping business practices. Further, the good employees are not over-burdened picking up after the laggards. In any organization, the good employees know who does not pull their weight and resent taking up the slack. I give as an extreme example a story from a business I later managed.

An employee, John (all names are changed), who had once been a star had just stopped performing, despite repeated discussions and warnings. Because John had previously been so valuable to the team and was in an important role, the General Manager and Regional President balked at firing John. Finally, they pulled the trigger.

> *"A system of bureaucratic rules subverts the ethics of freedom and responsibility that marks a culture of discipline."*
>
> *Jim Collins*

Several weeks later, the Regional President visited the plant and asked the controller how the business was surviving without John in his important role. Her response was tinged with sarcasm.

> Well, it has been very difficult for us to survive without John. But, we have done it. You see Ken now comes in late twice a week and then spends two hours talking by the water cooler. Mary comes to meetings late, contributes little and makes sarcastic comments. And I have been taking long lunches with my friends and charging it to the company as a sales expense. Yes, it has been difficult for us. But, by pulling together we have been able to cover and do all the work that John had done before.

The Organization is Leaner and Simpler

With accountability and execution required, bureaucracy and layers do not need to be added to keep tabs over employees and pound on them to do what they should be doing anyway. In reality, bureaucracy reduces accountability and responsibility by allowing blame to fall all too easily on "the system." Where there is less bureaucracy and fewer layers, the organization and business are simpler with a significant reduction in meetings, reports, reviews, etc.

Further, there is less, but more focused activity. Growth initiatives and profit improvement initiatives are undertaken only when there is accountability in the core business activities. As such, initiatives are only in place to move the business forward. In many unaccountable businesses, initiatives and consulting programs are really just substitutes for the lack of accountability currently in the business.

> As an example, if an "accountable" business had a sales problem, they would first make sure that they have the right sales team and right sales management in place and then hold them accountable before beginning a fancy sales improvement or sales training initiative.

Only when there is accountability throughout the organization, is it possible to determine the most important and highest leverage initiatives that would be worth the company's time and effort to focus on.

How to Over-Manage Accountability

As in everything, there is a balance. Some organizations push so hard towards accountability in every aspect of their business that they lose track of the overall goal of having the most successful business.

Too Lean and Mean

Jack Welch, the former CEO of GE, made headlines with his push towards differentiating employees and firing the bottom 10% of employees each year. As I have written about the widespread tolerance of non-performance, I believe that most companies do need to err towards letting go of non-performers sooner. But, a straight across the board commitment to terminating 10% of all employees is sub-optimal.

First, if everyone is performing and being accountable, why would you introduce the fear and inevitable politicking by decreeing that 10% will be fired anyway? It is naïve of any leader to think that such a policy will not create political and turf battles in the company and reduce the cooperation and teamwork.

Second, if more than 10% of your employees are not performing than you should address all of the non-performers, even if more than 10%, with the reassurance that if next year everyone performs than none will be fired.

Third, as I have mentioned before, compassion has to enter into any company's style of leadership. If a 64 year old and sick salesperson is working hard but only performing C+ work, then terminating him is likely to have negative consequences for morale and on-going performance. In creating an accountable and successful business, there is a balance between being too lenient and being too lean and mean. Being extreme in either direction is not optimal.

<u>Metrics Everywhere</u>

Some organizations pride themselves on being metric-driven; but this too can be taken to the extreme.

There are limits to metrics. In such grayer areas as new product development or R&D, accountability cannot be based solely on performance metrics and the end results because the end results are not guaranteed. There needs to be a focus on the effort, on doing what you said you were going to do, and on learning from past mistakes. Otherwise, all risk-taking will stop and innovation will be at risk.

> *"Be careful of what you measure, you may get it — and it may kill you. Complete focus on a metric is likely to improve the metric, but not necessarily the business."*
>
> **Michael Hammer**

Further, the goal of being accountable is to have the most successful business in the mid to long term. Focusing single mindedly on metrics may create short term victories at the risk of long term success ("widening the moat" as Warren Buffett wrote). And a relentless focus on metrics may often cause people to loss the focus on the broader goals of the business due to the constant attention on the metric. I give as an example a business that I visited.

> This business was a very profitable manufacturing business that prided itself on the quality of its operations. It was ISO 9001, lean, six sigma, etc. To get to this level of success, it had adopted a very clear system of about 20 metrics which it judged all operations on each and every day. Failure was not an option on any metric any time. Having 19 out of 20 metrics in line was still considered a failure. In touring the facility and spending time on the floor, I saw innumerable low hanging fruit: poor housekeeping, poor organization, poor

warehousing, and employees working at ¾ speed without any urgency or passion whatsoever. I asked the General Manager why he did not fix some of these obvious deficiencies. His response:

> Yes, we know about these issues. But, we have no time for training because we do not want to take anyone off the line. Training and correcting some of these problems would have a negative effect on the metrics in the short term. So we don't do them.

> As such, this business (which nevertheless remains successful) continues to run in a way that everyone from the General Manager on down knows is inefficient and less than optimal.

In summary, to be a well-led and well-managed business requires the business to have a well-balanced culture of accountability.

Chapter 19 – Motivate and Engage Your Team

> "You can't be a good leader unless you generally like people. That is how you bring out the best in them."

Richard Branson

- *Stop De-Motivating*
- *Start Leading*
- *Quiz*

A "Winning Business" is built by having talented, well-trained and engaged[8] employees. To that end, multi-billion dollar industries exist to help companies find the right talent and to teach, train, coach, and develop employees and managers.

Unfortunately, less time and money is spent ensuring that these same employees are motivated and engaged to give their best day in and day out. In a 2010 study by Towers Watson, an international HR consulting firm, fewer than 21% of employees surveyed described themselves as highly engaged, down from 31% in 2009.

---

8 I define an engaged employee to be someone who is both motivated and aligned to the goals of the business. Fully committed to his work, he strives to do whatever he can to further the success of the business.

Would having only one-fifth of your employees highly engaged be a hallmark of a Winning Business?

As an overview, employee motivation and engagement derives from three different factors:

1. **Alignment** of the employee with the values and goals of the business.

2. **Faith** of the employee in the competence and commitment of the business leadership to live the values and execute on the goals.

3. **Trust** in their direct supervisor that he will support his people and help them to succeed.

While many companies do a poor job of aligning their employees with clearly stated and well-communicated goals and a few companies have incompetent and uncommitted management, the overall cause of employee dissatisfaction and lack of motivation and engagement rests with the inappropriate behaviors and actions of employees' direct supervisors.

It has often been said that employees rarely quit companies. Instead, employees quit their managers or supervisors by leaving the company. Mark Herbert, a colleague who focuses on engagement, says:

> Motivation and engagement live and die on the front line of your business.

Increasing positive managerial behavior and reducing negative managerial behavior will go a long way towards improving employee engagement and motivating your team. When your talented employees are engaged, they are able to perform spectacularly and build and improve your winning business.

So, what do you need to do to improve the engagement, motivation and morale of your team?

Stop De-Motivating

The first thing that a leader should do to improve engagement and morale is to stop exhibiting de-motivating leadership behaviors.

<u>Don't Get Angry</u>
Mark Twain once said:

> Getting angry is easy. Anyone can do that. But getting angry in the right way in the right amount at the right time, now that is hard.

Anger is so hard to control that it should remain out of the managerial kit bag. Further, the old adage often applies: when you are truly angry you are angry at yourself. As a leader, your anger will inevitably be interpreted as being unfair. Where you may see just cause for your anger, your employees will likely see that you are angry at yourself for not communicating clearly or following up well. And they will feel, often quite correctly, that you are taking this anger out on them.

> *"Whom the Gods want to destroy, they first make angry."*
>
> **Ancient Greek Saying**

When you begin to get angry, force yourself to take a "cooling-off" period. A day or even a couple of hours will assuage a lot of your anger and allow you to be clear-headed in finding a resolution to what made you so furious. Using anger or the leadership style of "the beatings will stop once morale improves" all but assures that morale will not improve.

<u>Don't Be Cold, Distant, Rude or Unfriendly</u>
Especially in difficult times, employees take cues from their immediate supervisors and need to hear from them. Remember that

as a leader, you are always "on stage." As such, your team will judge you by your action, moods, and behaviors, not by your intent.

Don't Send Mixed Messages to Your Employees So That They Never Know Where You Stand

Keep your message simple and focused and prioritized on the most important things. Resist the urge to add just one more "really quick and easy" thing. Too many messages, too many initiatives, too many programs just confuse, alienate, and exhaust people. Less is More.

> I would generally visit with each of my General Managers once every two to three months. In each visit, I might meet with a customer, talk to the employees, and tour the plant. Inevitably, many issues would come up. My biggest struggle (which, I must admit, I would sometimes fail at) was to keep my overall message simple and consistent from visit to visit. I did not want to send mixed messages that would lead them to change their focus and priorities.

Don't BS Your Team

This includes saying things that you don't believe in. This includes hiding information and just plain lying. As mentioned before, our BS detectors are especially well-tuned with people in authority. Your employees may nod their heads and not tell you that it is BS (after all, you are their boss), but they will definitely know it for what it is.

Don't Act More Concerned About Your Own Welfare than Anything Else

Your success comes through the success of your team. So, work with your team to make them successful. "Self-serving detectors" are also very well-tuned in most employees.

> *"He that gives good advice builds with one hand. He that gives good counsel and example builds with both. But he that gives good guidance and bad example builds with one hand and pulls down with the other."*
>
> **Sir Francis Bacon**

Don't Avoid Taking Responsibility for Your Actions

You are the boss. As such, you are accountable and the buck stops with you. So, lead by your example. Accept responsibility for your mistakes.

Don't Be Hypocritical

You and your leadership team need to be governed by the same rules as everyone in the organization. So, follow the rules. This applies particularly today as many companies continue to have austerity programs in place. If that is the case in your business, you need to cut back on your perks and be visibly more cost-conscious.

> In the early 1990's, one business that I later led was struggling. Wages had been cut. Headcount and costs had been slashed across the board. A top corporate staff person was brought in to find ways to cut costs even more.   He led a number of meetings during his visit contributing cost-saving suggestions and advice. In the last meeting, he had to leave early. He had to rush to the airport to catch his $5000 Concorde flight to Europe.

Don't Be Petty

If your company has taken away employee privileges or cut the small things that just take away from employees without really saving significant money, stop it. Pay for the coffee service. Take an employee out for lunch on his birthday. Keep the tradition of Thanksgiving turkeys. Get someone to cut the grass or clean the office instead of having employees do it. Celebrate a big win with snacks and drinks. Yes, some of these cost money. And no, I am not suggesting that you bring in masseuses or start Friday Night Beer Pong. Just the basic conveniences for your team are important.

Don't Jump to Conclusions Without Checking Your Facts First

> *"See everything; overlook a great deal; correct a little."*
>
> **Pope John XXIII**

Get the facts and find the true truths from all concerned parties before acting.

> A few years ago, I watched in horror as a colleague approached an employee who had missed an important meeting that morning. The colleague was "loaded for bear" and started screaming the moment the employee arrived (so much for "Don't Get Angry"). After several minutes of verbal abuse, the employee responded: "I apologize and should have contacted you. But, I just got back from the hospital as my mother has been diagnosed with terminal cancer."

Don't Overmanage

Your talented people need to be given freedom to perform. Too much contact, too much criticism, too much "assistance" often inhibits and infuriates them. Yes, they will make mistakes and do things incorrectly, but you do not need to point them all out. Constantly doing so comes across as being sanctimonious and "wiser than thou." As the leader you do not have to be right all the time and you do not always need to get the last word in. For an aggressive leader, the hardest thing is often to see some small thing going wrong (in your opinion) and to not correct it. But, in order to accomplish the big things (build your team and business), we have to be able to let some small things go wrong.[9]

Start Leading

At the risk of repeating, increasing employee motivation and morale requires leaders to use the fundamental leadership tools.

Do What You Say

Doing what you say you are going to do when you said you were going to do it is essential. There is no better way to communicate the

---

9   Marshall Goldsmith's book, *What Got You Here Won't Get You There*, discusses the significant negative leadership behaviors and how to identify and correct them.

message that you are accountable for your promises and that everyone in your company should be accountable as well. As a leader, the key to developing trust and showing your integrity is to make and keep promises.

Be Responsive

Return phone calls, respond to E-Mails, and act decisively and quickly. As a leader, your team can be considered to be your customer. You want your sales team to punctually respond back to customer requests, so you should do the same. Further, by being responsive you avoid becoming the bottleneck and preventing your team from getting their job done.

Respect Your Team

Treat your team and your people with respect. Even the worst-performer is a human who deserves to be treated courteously and with dignity. In his book, *It's Your Ship*, US Navy Captain D.

> *"Fail to honor people, they fail to honor you."*
>
> Lao Tzu

Michael Abrashoff relates a study of reasons why sailors in the U.S. Navy were unhappy and did not re-enlist. The number one reason was "not being treated with respect or dignity."

Support Your People

"I've got your back" are four of the most useful leadership words. The team needs to realize that you support them not only when they are doing well, but also when they make mistakes. It is essential to publicly support your team. Your disagreements and disappointment with your employees can be communicated later and in private. Nothing appears as hollow as your attempt to blame your team for failures, especially in public.

Admit Your Mistakes and Take the Blame For Failures

As discussed in Chapter 11 on Honesty, your candor and ability to admit your mistakes helps the team realize that it is O.K. to try something and fail. Taking the blame for the team's failures is crucial to show everyone that you do not play the "blame game." You consider yourself (as you should) accountable for the team's performance, good or bad.

> *The best way to inspire people to a superior performance is to convince them by everything you do and by your everyday attitude that you are wholeheartedly supporting them.*
>
> **Harold S. Geenen,**
> **Former Chairman of ITT**

Recognize and Thank Your Team

The psychologist William James once said: "the deepest human need is the need to be appreciated." Recognize your team for what they have done well. Thank your team for all their efforts. You may have been instrumental in the success of the team. Nevertheless, be magnanimous and recognize and thank them for the success. Do it today.[10]

Ask and Listen

Employees have opinions and insights that they consider essential. As a leader, spend the time asking them for their views. Many years ago, Peter Drucker said:

> The manager of the future will know how to ask rather than how to tell.

The future is now. This is especially true with the younger generation of employees who have grown up accustomed to expressing their opinions and having them heard and validated. For a leader, some of the most dangerous words to say to your team would include: "But, you just don't understand…"or "Because I said so…"

Smile and Laugh

You should be having fun (most of the time). If you genuinely like people, then leading your winning team will be enjoyable. Show this

---

10   See the next Chapter for a more detailed discussion on recognition and appreciation.

enjoyment. But, be authentic; programmed fun and faked laughter from a curmudgeon is worse than doing nothing. When appropriate, laugh at yourself; it will humanize you.

Quiz

Please place these 10 items in order from most to least important for the average employee:

1. Good wages

2. Interesting work

3. Promotional growth in the organization

4. Job Security

5. Good working conditions

6. Personal loyalty to employees

7. Full appreciation of the work done

8. Sympathetic help on personal problems

9. Tactful discipline

10. Feeling of being in on things

No peeking at the answers. ☺

OK, are you done? Now, turn the page.

According to numerous surveys over the years, the order from most to least important for the average employee is as follows:

1. Full appreciation of the work done

2. Feeling of being in on things

3. Sympathetic help on personal problems

4. Job Security

5. Good wages

6. Interesting work

7. Promotional growth in the organization

8. Personal loyalty to employees

9. Good working conditions

10. Tactful discipline

Of course, you can quibble and debate about the order and the merit of any one survey. But, that is not the point. This is the point. You cannot promise job security. In today's economy, you may not be able to offer your employees a satisfactory raise in wages. And you should not guarantee personal loyalty. Nevertheless, you still have a lot of leadership and management tools at your disposal to improve the engagement and the motivation of the employees on your team. Use these tools and improve your employees' satisfaction, commitment and morale. Use these tools and make your team a winning team.

CHAPTER 20 – RECOGNITION

"You can never underestimate the power of
simple recognition for a job well done."

Anonymous

- *Why give recognition?*
- *How to give recognition?*
- *How to get started giving recognition?*

In the last chapter, we discussed the importance of having engaged and motivated employees on your winning team. Recognition is one of the most valuable leadership tools to build this engagement and motivation. Everyone on the team must feel that they are appreciated for what they do and thanked for doing a good job. In short, people want and need to be recognized.

Why Give Recognition?

<u>Giving Recognition Builds the Self-Confidence and Self-Esteem of Others on Your Team</u>
Even if you don't personally need to be recognized, most people do appreciate being recognized for the hard and good work that they are doing. There is ample research that people with more confidence in their job are more highly motivated and produce better work.

<u>Giving Recognition Creates a Winning Team Atmosphere</u>
Recognition is a positive in a world where we spend far too much time focusing on the negative. Think of winning teams in sports and the positive feedback and support you see them giving each other (high fives to the field goal kicker after he makes the field goal, etc.). Think of losing teams in sports and the negativity and lack of team spirit and appreciation of one another that is most often visible. Which culture do you want to foster?

<u>Recognition Helps Conquer Typical Friction Points in a Company</u>
Natural friction points abound in companies (sales v. operations, staff v. line, corporate v. field, etc.). By recognizing and being appreciative of the team members on "the other side," you will almost certainly see them be willing to go an extra mile to help you out. I give an example from one of my businesses:

> As a salesperson, Steve (not his real name) was always demanding of engineering and production. When they delivered on his requests, Steve said nothing or he would tell them that it was about time that they did what they were supposed to do. When they missed a deadline, Steve immediately complained to everyone and demanded action. Also in sales, Ben was always appreciative of engineering and production. He often commented and recognized them for their good quality and

responsiveness in sales reports and staff meetings. When they missed a deadline, Ben was demanding but respectful. He told them that he was disappointed, but he spoke with them directly.

Steve and Ben were equally good salesperson and equally good with the customer. Nevertheless, Ben was far more productive. His engineering and production requests always seemed to go to the top of the pile and be the first ones done. Meanwhile, Steve got little out of engineering and production; his requests always seemed to go to the bottom of the pile which only made him more vocal. In the end, Ben continued to have success and Steve was let go.

When I have told this story, a number of people have commented that it was not right to treat Ben and Steve's requests differently as both of them were just trying to do right for the customer. Perhaps. But, people are people and recognizing and thanking them makes people more responsive and helps build a sense of team spirit.

Recognition Allows for Candor and Honesty

When recognition is genuine, critiques (discussed later and separately) are more likely to be heard. Ben's less strident critiques when engineering or production made mistakes or missed a deadline were heard loud and clear and responded to. Steve's loud critiques were inevitably ignored. Likewise, as a leader, without positive encouragement and feedback, you are perceived as that "pigeon leader" who flies in with the white shirt, sh*ts on everyone, and flies back out. Since everything is always negative, nothing that the pigeon says is perceived as being constructive and is either ignored or done grudgingly. There is no motivation for the employees. The pigeon does not like anything or recognize anyone. So, the natural response of the employee is: why bother?

How to Give Recognition?

<u>Criticize in Private...Recognize in Private</u>

Group recognition means little to the individual. Think of the year end recognition at the company Christmas party:

> Thank you team. You have all done a wonderful job. Good work.

As the individual employee hearing that, that statement most likely means nothing to you; it is just empty words.

Further, with individual recognition in front of a group, those not being recognized feel slighted. "I would like to recognize Jane for her great work on this project." Kevin, Susan, and John, the other project managers who also do good work, each feel slighted and are likely thinking: "What am I, chopped liver?"

<u>Giving Recognition</u>

Step by step you should do the following:

1. Identify an opportunity for giving recognition

2. Describe the behavior as immediately and as specifically as possible

3. State how the behavior made a difference to you and to the organization and thank them for making that difference

It is best to give recognition face to face and then follow-up in writing. With this written follow-up, the recognition will resonate and mean much more. A simple example of giving recognition would be:

> Sarah, you did an excellent job to resolve Acme Corporation's problem.
> You were responsive throughout the process, zeroed in on the key

issue, and put the problem to bed quickly. As you know a satisfied customer is the lifeblood of our business. So, thank you for creating another satisfied customer. Today, you helped to make our company a little bit better and a little bit stronger. Well Done! And thank you again.

In giving recognition, be direct and genuine. Do not hem and haw. Do not say the word "but". If you feel that you must offer a critique as well, wait and give the criticism on another day. Otherwise, the critique will be heard and the recognition will be forgotten. In giving recognition, the sandwich method (a positive, a negative, a positive) does not work.

How to Get Started Giving Recognition?

<u>Find Someone Doing Something Right Every Day</u>
Starting today, create an action item for 20 minutes a day of MBWA ("Management by Walking Around") time. Interact with your team, thank them and give individual employee's recognition face to face when you see them doing something well.

If this is too difficult to schedule, then try the ten penny approach. As you walk into the office every morning, put the ten pennies that are piled up on your computer keyboard into your left pocket. Throughout the day, each time you give someone recognition or thank them for their work, move a penny from the left pocket to the right pocket. At the end of the day, take all ten pennies that are now in your right pocket and pile them up on your computer keyboard.

<u>Some Counter-Arguments Shot Down</u>
- *"I don't need recognition. So why do these others need it?"*

  First of all, you are not managing you. Second, do you really mean to say that it means nothing (absolutely nothing) to you when your boss or spouse gives you a compliment about something that you did?

- *"I try to do it. But, I just never get around to it."*

    Do it first thing, using the ideas from the section on finding someone doing something right every day.

- *"I have got a lot more important things on my mind."*

    Building and encouraging your team to be better is a pretty essential part of your job as a leader.

- *"Although the employee's work was good, it could be better. I will recognize them when their work becomes perfect."*

    O.K., so they still need to improve more. Well, how do you get them to improve? By doing nothing? Or by encouraging and supporting them? If you wait until everything is perfect, you may never give out any recognition at all. So, remember the old adage:

> The worst recognition that I ever got was the recognition that I never got.

<u>Just Do It!</u>

Giving recognition will brighten the day of the employees on your team and engage and motivate them to do even better. And by giving recognition, you will brighten your day. As Michael Bloomberg, the billionaire Mayor of New York City, says:

> In the end, everybody wants recognition and respect.

Chapter 21 – Continuous Learning

"It's what you learn after you know it all that counts."

John Wooden (UCLA Basketball Coach).

- *How not to do employee development*
- *Creating a learning culture*

The lessons in sport generally apply to the lessons in business. The best team wins. To get the best team, you have to have the best employees pointed in the right direction, ably led. And you have to have these employees keep getting better and better. In short, you need continuous learning within your organization.

How Not to Do Employee Development

The least effective way to train and develop your team is to throw money at your employees for seminars, executive education or tuition reimbursement and sit back satisfied that training has taken place.

In an all too common story, one business group required each profit center General Manager to spend a set amount of money on training

— approximately 1% of sales — as part of their bonus amount. As expected, the money was spent, often on expensive motivational speakers, and the bonuses were received. Unfortunately, the employees and the organization were not any wiser or stronger.

The unfortunate reality is that billions of dollars a year are wasted as corporations try to train and promote learning within their organizations. Inevitably, a leader will bring in a training firm or send employees for outside training. Unless the employee is fortunate to work in an organization that already values continuous learning, the lessons learned from these trainings will not last. The usual scenario is the following:

The institution doing the training has the best of intentions and has worked hard over the last several years to tie the training back to the specific job that the manager being trained is doing in his company. Nevertheless, at the end of the training, the manager goes back to his job. He has missed several days' of work and is behind. By the time, he has conquered that mountain and gotten caught up, the lessons learned at the course have begun to fade.

In many cases, the manager's supervisor sent the manager to the training because the supervisor either did not know how or did not want to directly train and develop the manager. As such, the supervisor never asks the manager what he has learned. If the supervisor does ask, he does not follow up to see what the manager is doing differently. Time passes, the daily grind continues, the ideas and insights from the course grow fainter and gradually disappear. In those cases where the manager does put the insights into daily use, they are added to an already full plate increasing the work load on everyone and reducing the probability that the insights will stick.

Yes, seminars, executive education and tuition reimbursement have a role to play in continuous learning. But, only within the context of a business which already has a culture of continuous learning in place.

Creating a Learning Culture

<u>Lead by Example</u>

A leader has to be (and be seen as) a learner. For many, this will be challenging. Today, many leaders have grown up and been successful in one environment and are finding it difficult to adapt to a new environment. As examples, think of how long it has taken some companies (especially B2B companies) to embrace the Internet and more recently social media. And consider how long it has taken leaders to adjust to the need for a focus on customers and growth as the heady days of economic prosperity are replaced by more challenging times.

It is challenging for a leader trained in one environment to thrive in another. But, it is essential. As the futurist Alvin Toffler writes:

> The illiterate of the 21st century will not be those who cannot read, but those who cannot learn, unlearn and relearn.

To show yourself as a learner:

- Show that you are willing to change yourself for the better.
- Show your curiosity and openness to new ideas. Seek out and experiment with new ways of doing things.
- Be actively networking with different people from different perspectives.
- Be actively up-to-date on the business, but also be reading different perspectives that others are not reading to broaden your vision.

Further, the business leader needs to encourage learning throughout the organization through his daily questions and follow-up.

First, when Managing by Walking Around encourage your

> *"Everyone thinks of improving the world, but no one thinks of improving himself."*
>
> **Leo Tolstoy**

employees to think and come up with better ideas: What improvements are you making? What new ideas have you come up with?

Second, require post-mortems on things good and things bad. A quick "lessons learned" on a successful project allows the team to learn what has been successful and apply these lessons to other parts of the business. A "lessons learned" on a failure can be even more powerful as it can help the team identify tell-tale warning signs and pitfalls in the future.   These post-mortems do not need to be long, ideally one page or less. But, they are vital learning tools.

> At the end of the year, I would require that each business unit write up a one page "lessons learned". What did you do well in the last year? What did you not succeed at and why? What new challenges or opportunities came up during the year? What are the goals for the next year? Sometimes, the answers were fluff and politically correct since this would be shared with top management. But, the usually candid responses helped the businesses identify systematic mistakes and weaknesses and see new critical issues that had arisen.

Finally, the business leader needs to share the new ideas and perspectives.

> I created a database of book summaries, good articles, and quotes[11] that I had collected over the years. I would usually send out to a General Manager or other employee when immediately relevant and when they had asked about it. This was an excellent reinforcement tool when combined with coaching. Seeing an article or comment from a respected source helped to support and corroborate what we had been discussing.

Today, such sharing of new ideas can be even more effective and less disruptive. It is possible to create a private learning website or

---

11   Where do you think I got all these quotes from? ☺

blog and promote the ideas through Twitter with a private feed.[12] This eliminates the large number of E-Mails that are sent out when someone in the group reads an interesting article.

But, don't over-do it. Truth be told, I have been guilty of being over-zealous in sending out too many articles or readings to my team. As I have come to realize, many of these unsolicited E-Mails become interruptions and distractions. They clutter In-Boxes and are not often read before being deleted and forgotten. As in all things, "Less is More." Aim for less frequent and more substantive sharing of ideas.

Assess the Learning Gaps

In training programs or workshops, assessments are rarely done to determine what people have learned and retained. It seems as though once we have graduated from school (be it high school, college, or graduate school), we have earned the right never to be tested on our knowledge and understanding again.[13]

Big Mistake!

I recommend both formal and informal testing to see the gaps in knowledge and thus prioritize the learning that needs to occur. I use both small quizzes and diagnostic tests. These assessments can be written, oral or a demonstration.

> *Through evaluating the learning gap, even veteran employees will recognize that they do not know it all and realize that there is still a lot that they should learn.*

---

12   With a private Twitter list, just tweet the article or post the short thought or comment. All these will collect in the Twitter stream for your group and be accessible to the group members when they have the time to read or reflect upon them (e.g. while waiting for an airplane). In this way, your leadership team can collect together the best of all the wide reading and learning of each member, significantly enhancing the team's collective learning and understanding.

13   Certainly, many companies test employees (especially incoming employees) on personality or critical thinking. But, rarely do they test on what someone knows.

Assessing the learning gap is important for several reasons. First, it clearly communicates what people know and do not know. Oftentimes, the knowledge gap is wider than expected.

> In the course of my Precast University sessions, I would give a rudimentary 12 question quiz on the company's products and services. The questions were some of the fundamentals that everyone from sales to production should have known. In giving it to more than 200 people, exactly one person got them all correct.

Second, it can humble people to realize that their understanding is significantly less than they expected.

Third, in the process of answering the questions orally, putting them down on paper, or demonstrating, employees often learn and commit the behavior or concept to memory. Finally, assessing the learning gap, gives talented people the impetus to learn and fill in these gaps.

> In our telecommunications business, I gave a written diagnostic test to all the salespeople, project managers and key management. The test covered:
>
> - Basic technical aspects of the product
> - What was the product line?
> - Uses of the product
> - Questions about the customer and their business
> - Questions about the competition
> - And some brief essays
>   - o Key selling features of our offering
>   - o Elevator speech (30 second pitch on why the customer should buy from you)
>   - o How to sell against the competition in a certain situation

The results were sobering. One person received a "B"; a few had "C's"; all others were "D's" or lower. In following up, a number of people mentioned that just answering the questions helped them to clarify their thoughts; some salespeople had never written down their elevator speech before or the key selling features.

After the test, the behavior of the team was gratifying. Most of the team began to realize that they did not know a lot of important information. So, they took the test and the answer key and begin to study it. Many began to ask question to really understand the technical aspects. Others began to collect data to learn more about the customers and the completion. And most of the sales team composed cheat sheets on selling features and re-drafted their elevator speeches to make them more effective. And, as a group, we created a written training and reference manual on the topics from the diagnostic test.

In short, assessing the learning gap can be a wake-up call for your team to realize some weaknesses and a catalyst for them to improve their understanding and subsequent performance.

Promote Peer to Peer Learning

A leader can have a significant teaching role; but that is only one part of the leadership tool-kit and cannot be over-used or its effectiveness will drop off. Moreover, as a leader, you do not understand the details of what most people are working on and cannot fully empathize with the daily challenges that your team faces. To have a learning organization, the employees on the team need to be learning from one another. They must learn peer to peer.

In working to implement peer to peer learning, we had a number of false starts and failures. The failures occurred when we basically shoved people

> *Before peer to peer learning can be effective, the employees need to develop personal relationships and feel that they are part of one team.*

together and told them to learn from one another and come up with best practices. In most of these cases, the people did not know one another except as a voice over the phone. There was no relationship and no trust. As such, the ego and pride of each individual would get in the way as each person tried to win and have more of his ideas included in the final compilation of best practices.

Peer to Peer Learning did work when the individuals had developed a relationship first. In my Precast University sessions, one of my main goals was to enable people from different plants (usually doing similar jobs) to get together and get to know one another. Dinners and events outside the class time were compulsory. "Girl-boy seating" was required everywhere; you could not sit next to anyone from your location or anyone that you knew well. The purpose of all of this was to get people to form relationships and know one another. From these relationships, they would begin to share information and lessons learned informally. They would begin to learn Peer to Peer.

To promote Peer to Peer learning, seek out ways and opportunities to get the team together to learn and share. This does not mean an expensive off-site team building event. It can be a simple "lunch and learn" session where different people teach or explain what they do on a daily basis.

Having a team member teach others is always effective. First, by preparing and then teaching the material, the person deepens his understanding of what he is teaching. Second, by teaching he has set a performance standard for which he will now be held accountable. Third, people in traditionally confrontational positions (e.g. sales v. operation) can see the other person's viewpoint and understand his priorities, thus aiding communication.

In addition, when someone went to a seminar or a training class, I would usually ask him to give a summary of the seminar, what he had learned, and what he would do differently. Often the individual would share the material from the class with his peers, allowing them to benefit as well.

At the senior level, I was perhaps most proud of the Peer to Peer learning that went on without my even knowing about it. Even though the General Managers and Presidents that worked for me were in different business, they would continually have discussion, share information, and learn from one another directly. Each one had realized that the others were substantial sources of ideas and learning that could be tapped to help him make his business better.

Tapping into the combined knowledge and expertise of the entire organization is the hallmark of a culture of continuous learning.

One final anecdote about Peer to Peer Learning:

> At our General Manager meetings, we developed the practice of having a session of "One Tough Question." In this session, I would sit in the back of the room and would not be allowed to speak. In turn, a General Manager would get up in front of the group, discuss a particularly vexing problem – the One Tough Question - that they were facing, and ask all the other General Managers for their thoughts and advice. As the "boss" of all these General Managers two things always stood out.

> First, nearly all the experienced General Managers had faced a similar situation, and it was great for each of them to realize that they were not alone. Second, the advice and experience of the other General Managers truly resonated with the General Manager with the Tough Question. In most cases, the General Manager would immediately act on the advice (which was often what they knew needed to be done but just had put off doing). Third and most relevant to our discussion in this part of the book, most of the "Tough Questions" revolved around people and the challenge of developing a Winning Team.

In conclusion, to develop a learning culture in your business, start today and think small. Learning takes place incrementally and builds on itself. Over time, small continuous learning gains are usually enough to help people improve their performance significantly and realize their goals.

Section V – Customer Service

CHAPTER 22 –
CUSTOMER SERVICE

"A customer is not dependent on us, we are dependent on him. A customer is not an interruption of our work; he is the purpose of it.

Leon Leonwood ("L.L.") Bean

The third fundamental of building a winning business is "Customer Service." All of us are customers in our lives, whether we are buying food, clothing, I-Pods, cars or services. As such, we are all well aware of the generally poor customer service from most businesses. In 1993, Ken Blanchard and Sheldon Bowles wrote the following:[14]

> Customers are often only satisfied because their expectations are so low and because no one else is doing any better. Perhaps, the customer service slogan should be: 'No Worse than the Competition.'

After eighteen years, billions of dollars spent in corporate training, and millions of customer service pledges, mission statements, and

---

14 *Raving Fans: A Revolutionary Approach to Customer Service* by Kenneth Blanchard and Sheldon Bowles

customer service guarantees, the situation has not improved. Most companies do not deliver superior customer service.

Before proceeding, let's step back and think about it for a moment.

- Who pays the paychecks of every employee in the company?
- Who provides the money that allows for positive cash flow?
- Who is the single most important reason that the business exists?

The answer, of course, is the customer!

To create true customer service and grow and build your successful business, you need to focus on three customer service keys:

1. Value your customer.

2. Satisfy your current customer's needs.

3. Grow outward from your customer base.

CHAPTER 23 –
VALUE YOUR CUSTOMERS

"If your business leader does not love customers and is not committed to delivering value to them, your venture will fail."

Ken Morse (Co-founder of 3Com
Corporation, Serial Entrepreneur)

- *Do You Value Your Customers?*
- *Customer Value Quiz*

A successful business leader needs to personally value the customer and realize the importance of each customer in building his business. Without his example, the organization will not value the customer and customer satisfaction will lag.

Personally valuing the customer is so important because finding and building a portfolio of customers is the most difficult thing for a business to accomplish. As such, it requires the time, attention, commitment, focus and passion of the business leader.

This is not an unequivocal defense of all customers. Doing business with customers can be difficult and challenging:

- Customers can be irrational and not know what they want.
- Customers can be demanding.

- Customers can be deceitful and lie.
- Customers do not always pay their bills.

Yes, all that can be true. There are bad customers out there as there are bad employees and bad people in general. Still, the challenge remains to satisfy and serve the right customers to build your business. Paradoxically, the poorer your customer service the more likely that you will end up spending time and effort with the wrong type of customers.

In short, your appreciation of your customers and focus on delivering value to them is a pre-requisite to creating a culture in your organization that leads to customer satisfaction, growth and success.

Do You Value Your Customers?

Quiz: Please answer the following one question.
- As a business leader, do you personally like being involved in sales and dealing with sales and marketing people and customers?

Being absolutely honest, the answer for many of you may be... **NO!** Ouch!!!

But, that is all right. You see I am a recovering customer phobe. At the beginning of my time as Division President, I did not value the customer and thought of the customer as a necessary evil that distracted me from all the other fun stuff in business (acquisitions, business turnarounds, operational improvement, start-ups, etc.). Fortunately, this lack of customer appreciation changed during the telecommunications bust when many of our then current customers literally disappeared overnight. Required to find new customers and markets to replace these lost customers and through the attentive nurturing of my two Sales and Marketing Vice Presidents[15], I was able to

---

15   Mike Flick and Rick Sauer

overcome my customer phobia and realize the value and importance of the customer. So, if I can change you can change as well.

If your answer to the question above was "No", great job and thank you for your honesty! You have taken the first step in realizing, acknowledging, and overcoming your customer phobia.

Hi, my name is David and I am a customer phobe…

Now that you have acknowledged it, you must figure out how to force yourself to spend the time with the customer and on customer service and sales issues. Without sufficient time spent focused on the customer, then your declaration that you value the customer will just be lip service.

You will need to change the way you do your job in order to spend the needed time on sales, customers, and growth. And yes, spending time on customer service may not appeal to the analytic, organized brain. There will always seem to be something more urgent to work on. Many sales calls will never lead any further and thus appear to have been useless wastes of time.

> *"The customer should be the center of any company's universe."*
>
> **Tom Steenburgh, Harvard Business School**

The easiest way to re-prioritize on the customer is to commit to some set amount of time each day, say two hours. Make this commitment public to others in your organization to give you the extra incentive to do what you say to avoid losing face. Then, follow through on your commitment and track your time every day. If it remains difficult to find the time to do the two hours every day, re-jigger your schedule and get this important task done first.

- Spend time meeting with customers for breakfast
- Discuss customer service issues first thing in the morning
- Focus on the customer before you do anything else in the day, before you read your E-Mails, before you respond to phone calls, before…

Alas, if you remain unwilling to commit your time and effort to the customer, customer service and sales, please re-read the quote from Ken Morse (an analytical MIT grad for heaven's sake) or ask other successful business leaders for their advice.

Customer Value Quiz

For those of you who are still with me, let's have another quiz about valuing customers to see how loudly our actions as leaders are speaking:

Quiz: Please answer the following three questions.

1. **How many customer service problems has your company had in the past month?** Which type of problem is most prevalent? Product defects? Missed customer deadlines?

2. **How many times have you personally been in front of a customer in the past month?** To resolve a customer service issue and personally apologize? To visit with a good and satisfied customer to thank him for his business and ask how you can serve him better?

3. **How many times have you attended a sales meeting in the past month?** To go through your sales team's activity reports asking about who is buying and why? To find out from the sales team about unsatisfied customers? To find out where the sales team is being successful or unsuccessful in the market and against the competition?

I would daresay that many of us have incomplete answers to these three questions. If so, then we know where we need to begin to better value and focus on the customer.

CHAPTER 24 – SATISFY YOUR CURRENT CUSTOMERS' NEEDS

"At Zappos, we try to see customer service not
as a cost, but as a powerful marketing tool to
differentiate our business from everyone else."

Tony Hsieh (CEO, Zappos.com)

- *The importance of customer satisfaction*
- *Fun facts about customer satisfaction*
- *Seven steps to customer satisfaction*

As discussed in the previous chapter, the initial step in successful customer service is to have the business leader visibly respect and value the customer. The second step is to satisfy the needs and exceed the expectations of current customers.

The Importance of Customer Satisfaction

In general, tremendous attention is dedicated to the "sexy" business of finding new customers and markets. Yes, that is critical and is part of the third stage in customer service and growth. However, much of that effort is wasted if the success in finding new customers and markets only replaces the revenue that was lost as your current customers stopped buying from you.

To grow, you first need to master the "mundane" task of holding on to your current customers by satisfying them and keeping them buying.

To highlight this importance, I relate a story from my own experience.

> A few years ago, a $10M operation became part of my division. As a way to re-charge growth, I began working with the General Manager and the team to re-establish the importance of the customer and customer service. I asked the General Manager to go out and start talking to customers (both current and former). A few weeks later, the General Manager called to tell me about a meeting that he had just had with one of their former customers. The General Manager had met with the President of the customer company. This company, which was one of the three largest potential customers in the market, had done business exclusively with our operation until about five years before.
>
> In excruciating detail, the customer President told the General Manager the story of why they stopped buying from us. Our company had let the customer down on a critical and time-sensitive job. Our product was late; we then lied directly to the President about the shipping status of the product costing the customer more money and delays; we never followed up; and we certainly did not apologize for our mistake.
>
> It was no surprise that that was the last order our company had gotten from that customer. In our discussion, my General Manager and I determined that this atrocious customer service and lack of follow-up had cost this $10M operation about $7.5M in revenue over the previous five years – approximately 15% of its actual revenue during that time.

Think of the time and effort that went into getting new customers to replace the revenue lost by this one customer's dissatisfaction. In short, current customer satisfaction matters.

Fun Facts about Customer Satisfaction

A survey conducted in the early 2000's about customer satisfaction had the following results:

- It costs five times more to attract new customers versus keeping old ones.
- 68% percent of the customers who walk away, do so because of lack of attention and follow-up after the sale.
- The average customer tells nine to ten other people about a poor service experience.
- But, most customers will repeat buy if they feel that their customer service issue was resolved satisfactorily. And they will tell five to eight people about the good service that they received.

Again, you can quibble about the precision of the survey. But, the gist is clear. Growth for your business starts with your current customers.

Seven Steps to Customer Satisfaction

1. Measure Your Churn and Act On It

Measure your customer turnover (churn) over the last few years. How many customers have you lost over this time? How many customers are buying less and less often from you? Then, follow up. Don't accept the answer that your customer's business is smaller. Ask them why they stopped buying or are buying less. And work to earn back their trust and get them back into the habit of buying from you.

2. Institute a Simple Customer Satisfaction Survey

GE and others have used a two question customer satisfaction survey with success:

1. On a scale of 0 – 10, how likely are you to recommend this supplier to other people
   a. 0 – 3: Negative
   b. 4 – 7: Neutral
   c. 8 – 10: Positive

2. Do you have any comments or suggestions for ways that we can serve you better?

The key is to make this survey or any survey as easy to respond to as possible. Alas, many companies try to make it easier for them to collect and collate the survey results while making it harder and thus less likely for the customer to respond. Stick the short survey in an

> *"How many customers did we fail to satisfy yesterday?"*
>
> **Howard Lester of Williams - Sonoma**

E-Mail and ask the customer to answer the questions and hit the Reply button. Personally, I am glad to respond to a survey like that. It takes me two minutes and I get a chance to share my thoughts. But, I rarely click on a hyperlink to take me to a survey. It takes too much time, and I dread that the survey is going to be 30 questions long.

3. Lead By Example on Customer Service
   Get actively involved in customer problems and issues to understand and resolve their problems and issues.

> In his effort to transform IBM into an integrated, customer-friendly organization, Lou Gerstner required his top 200 executives to make face-to-face problem-solving visits to at least five customers each, and then get personally involved in every visit report.

Further, teach and preach customer service. Autopsy customer service failures and publish the lessons learned. Share and praise your customer satisfaction success stories.

4. Treat Your Customers Well

Respect the customer. There are no irrational customers, only lazy and arrogant suppliers. The customer may be doing something that makes no sense, but he will always have a reason for it (trying to save face and blaming someone else for his own problems are certainly common). It is your job to realize these reasons and respond to them appropriately. Further, even when the profit on a sale is low, the customer expects and deserves good service.

Communicate with the customer. Return their phone calls and respond to their E-Mails. Even if you do not have the answer, tell them that you received their message and will get back to them by a specific date. As I mentioned before, be honest with the customer. If there may be problems, give the customer a "flashing yellow light" as a heads up so they know and can prepare for what might be coming next.

5. Perform

Performance is simple: do what you say you are going to do. Further, ensure that what you are providing matches the expectations of the customer, delivers on the customer's hot buttons, and solves the custom-

> *The best thing that any company can do today to grow their business is to exceed the expectations of every customer that they interact with today.*

er's problem. It is important to realize that the customer's expectations may be different from what the purchase order or the contract says. But, unless you find out what their expectations really are and manage them, you risk having an unsatisfied customer.

6. Maintain a Sustainable Presence With the Customer and In the Marketplace

With your sales team and others, establish consistent and intelligent customer contact and follow-up. At the same time, don't waste the customer's time. If the customer does not buy during a sales call, try to give them a little quid pro quo (perspective, advice, industry overview, leads, etc.) and get out.

Listen to the customer during all sales calls and follow-up. In a survey by *Harvard Business Review,* it was determined that what customers most wanted was a sales person that understood the customer's problems and understood how the salesperson's product and services could help the customer resolve these problems. To understand the customer's problems, requires you to talk less about your company, your products and how great they all are. Instead, ask and listen. In listening, clarify and confirm what the customer has said. This will show your interest and show that you care. To repeat, the customer is only listening to one radio station: WII-FM (What's In It For Me).

Maintain a continuous presence in the marketplace as well. You need a constant (if not excessive) marketing campaign that brings attention to your company, your products and your progress. You cannot abandon a market segment and then return back to it when your other work dries up. If you are going to be in a market segment, you need to visibly be present in that market segment for the long haul.

7. Get Close to the Customer

As we will discuss in the next chapter, get close to your customer to ask about other needs and requirements that your company can address with them: opportunities for additional sales; ideas for new products and services; the possibility of a partnership with the customer potentially tying you in closer with them.

> *"Companies need to be closer to their final customers in order to hold them, to upsell them, to cross-sell them, and to garner high margin follow-on sales."*
>
> **Michael Hammer**

Think about it. Your current customers already have a habit of giving you money. If you continue to earn their trust on a daily, weekly, monthly, yearly basis by doing what you said that you were going to do, nearly all of them will remain loyal. With loyal current customers, all the work to win new customers and penetrate new markets will be an add-on to your current revenue stream.

Chapter 25 – Grow Outward from Your Customer Base

"Be focused like a hedgehog.... What can you be the best in the world at? What drives your economic engine? What are you deeply passionate about? At the intersection of these three circles is where you should focus your efforts."

Jim Collins

- *Why pursue growth*
- *Expand outward from your current customers*
- *But, what about acquisitions?*

Why Pursue Growth?

"I have a nice business and I am making a nice profit, why can't I just stay the same size, continue to service my good customers, and continue to make the same profits? In short, why do I need to grow?"

Good question.

The simple answer is that businesses must be constantly pursuing new customers and seeking out market opportunities just to stay even over the long haul. Customers and markets change so rapidly that no company can rest on its laurels without risking stagnation and eventual decline. Think of the companies and the industries that are declining or have declined into oblivion: countless computer companies (Digital Equipment, Packard Bell, and Gateway), Blockbuster and video rental stores, the record industry and the music store, and local telephone service. I experienced this personally in the supposedly slow changing infrastructure business.

> In 2000, one business had a record year with sales in excess of $30M. The business was diversified with five distinct market segments and leading market positions in all segments including sole source in two. Just five years later, the business reality had changed dramatically. The economy was even more robust in 2005 than in 2000. And the business still had its leading and sole source market position in each segment. Nevertheless, the sales from the customers and markets that the business had in 2000 had declined to a little more than $8M by 2005. Without our efforts in the previous five years of penetrating three new market segments, the business would have collapsed and been deeply in the red.

In short, all businesses need to continue to find ways to grow into new market segments and with new product and service offerings.

Expand Outward From Your Current Customers

My colleague Pete Kelly taught me to "grow the business from the inside out." You build upon the success with current customers as discussed in the previous chapter. And then you pursue opportunities in the same market space with new customers. You then pursue new market opportunities with the same customers.

Finally, you branch further afield pursuing new market and product opportunities.

> *"Highly focused companies — those with a small number of strongly positioned businesses — did much better than diversified companies over the last decade. Suggestions to match these successful companies include…finding profitable opportunities within the boundaries of current operations."*
>
> **Bain and Company Study**

I. Exceed the expectations of current customers to increase share of wallet with these customers.

2. Increase your market share with your current product line in that same market space.

3. Work with your current customers to determine new product and service opportunities.

4. Pursue new market opportunities already under your nose.

5. Actively pursue new market and product opportunities.

Before, we get started I have a word of caution. My experience is that most business leaders spend a tremendous amount of time and effort on pursuing new market and product opportunities (number five) while their true growth comes from the first four points. I have done this as well.

> While managing the telecommunications equipment shelter business, our original product line and customer base continued to decrease as the bubble deflated and the market changed. In response, we worked all five stages of the growth platform and were able to roll-out many successful new product and service offerings and penetrate into five

new market segments. In total, we increased annual sales of these new products and services from $4M to $44M for a $40M increase.

During this time, we had at least one full-time person and sometimes a team of people devoted solely to the active pursuit of new market and product opportunities (Growth Step #5). In doing this, we easily spent more than a million dollars.

- We partnered with small entrepreneurial start-ups with truly innovative and game-changing products.
- We produced countless full scale prototypes and two patented products.
- We researched, analyzed and tried to enter about a dozen other market segments.

In the end, all this development work never contributed more than $2M in annual sales growth. Of course, we were not perfect at how we went about pursuing this new product and market development. But, still think of the difference between $38M in growth for the first four steps and $2M in annualized growth for Step #5.

I. Exceed Expectations of Current Customers

In the previous chapter, we talked about satisfying and exceeding the expectations of your current customers. This is the single most important thing that you can do to re-charge the growth of your business. Full stop.

By this consistent performance, you build relationships with the customer. As a mentor, the late Jack Baker, once told me:

> Do what you say and when you say it. If you are going to be late or have made a mistake, notify the customer. This builds confidence which builds trust which builds lasting relationships.

With these strong relationships, your customers will support you in many ways. Most importantly, you will increase your market share with that customer. Further, they will often provide information and market data, introduce you to other potential customers, and bring you in to help them on additional problems that they might be having.

This daily work of executing on customer satisfaction may be "un-sexy", but it remains fundamental to your success.

2. Increase Your Market Share

As you have continued success with your current customers, you will seek to increase your market share in that same market space with new customers. A full discussion of how to increase market share would justify one complete book, in and of itself. It would include having the right leadership, the right marketing, the right sales management, and the right salespeople who understand the customer's problems and propose the right and well-priced solution to these problems. To keep within the scope of this book, I will consider two ways (often over-looked in the B2B world) to increase market share: viral marketing and leveraging a strong brand image.

- *Viral Market Out to New Customers*

I have worked in numer-ous industries — telecommu-nications equipment, building materials, environmental, auto-motive supplier. In every case, people comment on how small an industry it is and that every-

> *"Customers are three times more likely to trust peer opinion over marketing or advertising in their purchasing decisions."*
>
> **Jupiter Research**

one knows one another. In many ways that is true; the universe of people involved in the specific purchasing side of these industries is small and these people often move from company to company.

As you try to establish new customer relations in your current market space, the reputation of your company will precede you. Once you have established a positive reputation in the marketplace, you will be able to build on this reputation by getting referrals and viral marketing out to new customers in the market space.

Let me give an example.

> For our infrastructure product and services business with the cable television industry, we would generally start with one regional manager at one company. Once we had knocked the ball out of the park on our work for him, this manager would refer us to managers in other regions

of his company, increasing our share with the company overall. Then, when one manager shifted to a competitor (which often happened), they would bring us in and the cycle would start all over again.

Moreover, these customers understood that they could rely on us for any of their infrastructure requirements. As such they asked us to assist on numerous different issues that were outside our previous experience (e.g. providing relief after hurricanes and natural disasters), but integral to our goal of becoming a partner to our customers for any of their outside plant infrastructure needs.

This is the essence of viral marketing, relying on word of mouth, referrals and recommendations of satisfied customers to build the business. We grew this business from nothing to $25M in five years. The General Manager of the business, Dan Baker, and I would joke that building the business through viral marketing was...

...really like the 1980's Faberge Organic shampoo commercial with Heather Locklear. We got our satisfied customers to tell two friends who told two friends who told two friends and so on and so on.

To viral market well, you must first perform. Then, ask your satisfied customer for recommendations and referrals. Of course, your customers are not going to give you their direct competitors, but they will likely know many others in the industry that would need your products and services and do not directly compete with their company. Today, Linked In makes this referral process even easier as you can find out who else your good customer knows in his and related industries. Finally, if your satisfied customer is unwilling to offer a recommendation or referral you may need to consider whether they are as satisfied as you thought.

- *Build and Leverage Your Brand Image*

By now, my marketing focused readers must be at the boiling point.

> David, you stupid @*$&#*, you have been talking for quite a while about customer service and growth and you have not yet talked about marketing and the brand!

That would be correct. I have not yet talked about marketing and brand on purpose. The goal of your branding and your marketing effort is to tell customers and potential customers what your company is about, what makes it unique and better, and why they should do business with you. Unless you are already exceeding customer expectations and benefitting from viral marketing, any branding and marketing campaign would not be in alignment with the reality of what you are delivering and what you can deliver.

> *The more satisfied customers that you have, the stronger your brand becomes. The stronger your brand, the easier it becomes for you to be the recognizable, easy and first choice for solving the customer's problem.*

> Several years ago, I worked with one of my companies as it began to develop a marketing and branding campaign. The General Manager, the Vice President of Sales, and I all spent time reviewing customer service issues, speaking with customers, and meeting with the sales team. It soon became apparent that we had a lot of work to do before we could begin to market and brand ourselves. We agreed that if we were to market and brand ourselves right then and there, the only truthful branding tag line would have been:

> Buy from us. We suck, but we suck less than everybody else.

What is a Brand?

A brand is a statement of the identity or image for your company, product, or service. The brand is your determination of what makes your product unique and what it stands for. A successful brand will:

- Strengthen awareness and recognition of your company, product or service.
- Create positive attitudes and perceptions in customers' minds.
- Build and maintain trust that your company will deliver on the promise implicit in the brand.

In B2C (Business to Consumer), the brand is (and has long been) a vital component of all sales and marketing efforts. The Nike Swoosh™, the Coke™ brand, and the Apple™ brand are literally worth billions of dollars each to their respective companies. Brands matter in B2C because it is impossible to reach directly all the possible customers for your particular product or service. As such, marketing and brand building are done with the objective "to make selling superfluous."[16] That is, to get new customers to buy for the first time and to remind current customers to repeat buy.

In B2B (Business to Business), sales and marketing usually involve direct sales efforts, trade shows, and marketing literature. Historically, the power of a B2B brand is often an after-thought. Yet, a strong company or product brand is a vital part of a B2B sales and marketing effort, especially in attracting new customers for the first time.

- Think of your own experience if you are going to buy a business product or service for the first time. As you search the Internet or thumb through a buyer's guide, you have many choices. Everyone claims to offer quality, value and service; but, you do not believe any of it. Who do you buy from? Most likely, the company with the brand name that you trust or, at the very least, that you recognize.
- Think of IBM in the mid-1970's to the mid-1980's. The power of IBM's B2B brand was summarized in the expression: "you will

> never get fired for buying a computer system from IBM." Think
> of the billions of dollars in effortless sales that this statement
> and IBM's brand recognition brought to IBM.

With an effective brand, customers pick up the phone and contact you first. If you can service them effectively, they are unlikely to go anywhere else.

Branding matters now more than ever. With today's biblical flood of information, marketing hype and communication, the real challenge is to get your message heard: to get your company or product known and established and to get others to listen to you. As Dan Gilbert, the CEO of Quicken Loans, says:

> The most difficult aspect of growing your business is just getting
> people to pay attention. It's seventy percent of the battle.

A strong brand aids you in this battle for attention. To build an effective brand for your product or business, you will need to stick, align, and deliver:

Create a "Sticky" Brand Image

The key to any brand, marketing material, tag line or company image is to be understandable and memorable – to "stick." You want the brand to lodge itself in the customer's skull and stay there.[17] A sticky brand is:

- **Simple.** The brand needs to be short and simple. As such, it should contain only the core promise targeted to the audience you are trying to reach. While you may be able to solve a broad array of problems, you need to focus the brand message on what you do best and what is in the best interest of your audience. The goal is not to be front of your customer's mind all the time; the goal is to be front of mind when they are looking for the solution that you can best provide. Finally,

---

17   This concept of "stick" come from *Made to Stick: Why Some Ideas Survive and Others Don't* by Chip and Dan Heath.

keep it simple and communicate in language that can be understood by an eighth grader.

- **Concrete.** Be specific and targeted to how you can help solve the targeted customer's problems. As an example, the FedEx brand focused on the customer and tells you exactly what problem FedEx can solve:

> When your package absolutely positively has to be there overnight.

Further, create a brand message that is tangible and, if possible, visible. Avoid abstract words. Avoid ambiguous words that cannot be defined and measured (value, quality, reliability, etc.). And avoid words that have lost all sense of meaning – synergy, solution provider, one-stop shop.

> *"A strong brand promise makes it clear what to say 'No' to – saying yes to everything means you stand for nothing with high costs."*
>
> **Rick McPartlin**

- **Credible.** It needs to be believable that you can deliver on the brand promise. Focus on the core promise of what you can deliver, and do not over-promise. As an example, Southwest Airlines is the "low fare, reliable and fun airline." It is not the "low fare, highest quality, and most luxurious airline." As customers ourselves, we are always suspicious when someone is promising too much. Do we really believe the never-ending promises and guarantees in a 2:00 am infomercial?

- **Vivid.** Finally, make your brand come alive. To do so, back your brand with stories. Stories are memorable and thus stick in the customer's mind; stories add a personal touch. Tell stories that match up with your brand and describe how your company solved other customer's problems and helped them to succeed. And to enhance your credibility, admit your mistakes and tell stories about how your company failed and then recovered. Especially in the B2B world, customers know that mistakes happen. They are often tolerant of those mistakes if they have been properly communicated to and if the supplier corrects itself and delivers in the end. A colleague Paul McGhee explains the power of stories:

> Selling is asking the right questions. Selling is listening. And selling is telling the right stories. Some stories are best told with pictures, some with numbers, some with analogies, some with comparisons, some with customer quotations, some with 3rd party data and some with internally observed metrics. You don't tell every story every time. But if you tell the right stories at the right time in the right way, you win more. And if your entire sales team is telling the right stories, you win a lot more.

Creating a sticky brand image is hard work. But, it will be effective in getting your message across and getting heard.

Align Your Company to Deliver

As discussed in Chapter 14, having your employees aligned with your values and goals is essential. Likewise, it is important that your employees are aligned to fulfill the message implicit in your brand. After all, it will be your employees and your team that will ensure that your company will or will not deliver on the brand promise. The goal is to have everyone from the top down keep the brand and the brand promise front of mind.

To see how well aligned your company is, try a little poll in your company. Ask employees at all levels of your company two questions:
- What is the brand statement of the company?
- What does this brand statement mean to you in your day-to-day job?

You may get a lot of different answers on question number one and a lot of blank stares on question number two. What is needed is to have everyone know what the brand statement is, know how important it is to the company, and know what they need to do in their jobs to ensure that the company delivers on the brand statement.

Think of FedEx once again. While FedEx is certainly not perfect, their brand promise has been infused through the company well enough that any front-line employee knows that if he has to choose between spending an extra $50 or jeopardizing the overnight delivery of a truckload of packages, he would spend the extra $50. This is the alignment that is required to deliver on your brand promise.

Marc Benioff, CEO of Salesforce.com, puts it this way.

> People who work for you represent your brand. You want them to present themselves, and represent you, in a certain way. Whether employees realize it or not, everyone in a company interfaces with customers in one way or another, and their attitude will affect the brand. That's why we work so hard to make sure we have the right people representing our brand, and that everyone is in alignment once they get here.

Deliver on the Brand Promise

The key element in any brand is trust; trust that your company, product or service will deliver on the brand promise. Without delivering on the brand promise, the trust is lost and the brand loses value rapidly.

- What would be the value of FedEx's brand if it only successfully delivered 50% of its packages in the time promised?
- What is happening to the value of the Toyota brand as recalls continue and quality problems persist?

In monitoring your delivery on the brand promise, ask some questions:

- Are your employees aligned to deliver on the brand promise?
- Is the promise implicit in your brand considered to be one of the top priorities in the company?

- Do you measure how often you fail to live up to that brand promise?
- Are you listening to your customers (directly and through social media) to understand how they perceive your brand?

If you did not answer yes to all four questions, you are in danger of not fulfilling the brand promise to your customer. As such, you are at risk of losing the trust of your customers. This put you in danger of being perceived as just another company that talks a good game, but does not deliver.

All of your marketing, advertising, and brand building, brilliant as they may be, will be for nothing, if you do not deliver as a company on your brand promise. To paraphrase Ralph Waldo Emerson:

> Your company's actions (in delivering on the brand promise) speak so loudly that your customer cannot hear what you are saying.

But What About Social Media?

Marketing is changing as we speak. The traditional B2B marketing tools — trade shows, marketing literature and brochures, advertisements in trade journals, web sites — are all significantly less effective than in the past. All of us have been so overwhelmed by the daily overflow of advertisements and marketing pitches that we believe few of them and act on none of them. As such, stories, relationships, thought leadership and expertise have become the more effective marketing tools. Social media, be it Blogs, Linked In, Twitter, or Facebook, facilitate just such marketing.

While a full discussion of social media and social media marketing is outside the scope of this book, I summarize three key benefits of Social Media in improving customer service for your B2B business.

Build your brand

Social media helps to increase the visibility and enhance the perception of your brand. Through blogging, tweeting (Twitter) and a strong presence on key Social Media sites, you can increase your visibility to build your brand. Through blogging, you can tell stories and share information that reinforces your key brand promise showing how your company lives its brand promise. Finally, these stories personalize and humanize your company and brand.

Further relationships

Social media helps you and your team to make and maintain more business relationships. Through Facebook, Linked In and engaging in conversations within social media, you can expand your network getting referrals to customers and other people whom you want to know. Social media allows you to facilitate relationships by knowing more about the people you meet creating more immediate commonality with them.

Information

Social media can improve the information flow between you and your customer. Through blogging and tweeting, your company can share information that shows your customers and potential customers that you know what you are talking about and understand and care about their needs and the issues that they face in their marketplace. Through Facebook and following the blogs and tweets of your customers, you can listen to what your customers and others are saying about you and your brand.

3. <u>Work with Your Current Customers to Determine New Product
    and Service Opportunities</u>

Your satisfied customers are a gold mine of information if you
are listening to them. If you pay attention they will give you a deeper
understanding of their industry and your competitive position. They
may tell you about:

* Upcoming changes at their company
* Changes at other companies in their industry
* New competitors in their industry
* The future direction of the industry
* Strengths and weaknesses of your direct competition
* Emerging competitors in your own industry

All of this information is invaluable in helping you grow and
improve your business. If your salespeople are not getting this feedback, train them how to ask and listen better. Further, get out into
the field, speak with customers, and get this information yourself.

> In going out to visit with customers, I continued to be surprised at
> how flattered the company was that I wanted to meet with them
> and thank them for their business. In their minds, I was the "big
> boss" and they really wanted to get to know me as I represented the
> company. The discussions usually evolved to a discussion about
> business values and business in general, which would allow me to
> understand the customer and learn a great deal about the competi-
> tive situation. This was not due to my brilliance (or lack thereof) as
> a salesperson or conversationalist. Rather, many customers like to
> know who the final decision-maker really is and to judge whether that
> person can be trusted.

Once a customer realizes that you are an excellent and reliable
supplier, they will often bring you into other related parts of their
business where they may be having issues. Further, good customers
will team with preferred suppliers in refining current products and
services or in solving new problems that they may be facing.

Teaming together has two benefits. It ties you together more closely, and it gives you an improved product or a new product line that you likely can (with minor revisions) sell to other customers. Initially, you may be donating your time and expertise. Think of it as a quid pro quo to increase your visibility and tighten your relationship with the customer. But, over time and as the cost of the development increases, most good companies will commit funds to help you defray the development expenses. I have seen this happen in virtually every industry that I have worked with: telecommunications, space and defense, automobile, building materials, utilities, alternative energy. When the product development or refinement becomes successful, you will have significantly enhanced your relationship with that core customer. Further, even if the customer cannot sole source, any resulting specification will be written around your design putting you in the driver seat to win the work.

Some objections that you may have:

- **My customers never want to do this.** Have you asked them how you can improve the product and service that you supply? Have you offered to team up with them?
- **My customers do not want to team with us.** If they want to team with a competitor, then, most likely, that competitor has a superior relationship with that customer.
- **My customers want me to pay all the expenses.** If the product improvements and refinements are something that the customer really values, then they will begin to pay for it. If they do not want to pay at all, you should evaluate whether it makes sense to continue. Sometimes, the threat of you stopping work is enough to get the customer to commit some money. Other times, I have seen where your development work with a customer just becomes a pet project of some staffer within the customer company to justify his job. It is vital to identify this and cut the cords before the project becomes a sink hole of time and money.

In 2007 alone, my division worked with customers in the wireless, cable television, environmental, and the alternative energy markets on new product development and product enhancements. In each case, the customers paid a fair share of the expenses and committed significant time towards the project. At the same time, we began a project in the Homeland Security area where we were never paid and reimbursed. In mid – 2008, far too late, we pulled the plug on this project. Later, we learned that we had never been considered more than an alternative to allow the customer to have the legally required three bidders even though they knew who they were going to choose all along. We learned an expensive and time-consuming lesson. In most cases, if the customer will not contribute money, the project is just not important enough to them.

4.   <u>Pursue Market Opportunities Already Under Your Nose</u>
As a business successfully serving customers, numerous new product and market opportunities come into your company each day.

• *Mine your Data*
Your information system is another gold mine of marketing data.
First, consider the positive side of the customer turnover (churn) data that you collected in Chapter 24. Consider new customers and customers that are now buying more from you than in the past.

- Why are they now buying from you?
- Who are the decision-makers in these companies?
- Are they using your products in different ways than your other customers?
- What industries or markets are they in? Are there other companies in those markets that might want your products or services?
- Do they represent different end users?

Next, ask the same questions about new companies to whom you have quoted but lost. Also, try to determine why you might have lost. Finally, for all customers determine where your margins are highest and where your win ratio is highest. Why? Do these represent market areas that would be fruitful to pursue more aggressively?

> In achieving our business development success, we begin by developing a detailed quote tracker system that was not currently in place at the time, but is now available on most company data systems. We tracked all the data about our quotes: customer, product or service, location, customer industry, who the end user was (when it was not the customer), the end user industry, the key people in the decision making process. Using this data gave us great detail into who was buying our products and services and why. As an aside, the most difficult, but also most valuable, data was determining the end user in the cases where the customer we dealt with was between the end user and us. Getting this data was crucial to know who the final consumer was. By getting closer to that "consumer" we were able

to see new uses and markets for our products and services that we had not previously thought of.

- *Be Open to New Customers*

Most likely, a number of potential new customers are contacting your business today to see if you can help solve their problems. How will these potentials be treated?
    - Will your company's professionalism show through?
    - Will they get the answer that they are looking for?
    - Will their phone calls or E-Mails be returned?

In our lives as consumers and customers, all of us are aware of how difficult it is, at times, to buy from companies. As a business leader, foster the culture of "being easy to do business with" to avoid driving away the potential customers who have already taken the initiative to contact you.

- *"You Can Always Say 'No' Later"*

Take it a step further. Work with the companies that contact you looking for a solution to their problem. I have seen (and been guilty myself) too many times where businesses get contacted by a company with a request that is slightly out of the norm and reject it because it is too much work or they don't have time.

> A few years ago, I met a potential customer at a local networking event. After we got to know one another, he remarked that his company purchased a lot from our local competitor. I asked him why he had not considered buying from our company, especially as we were well-established in the market. His response was sobering:
>
> > Oh, I tried to buy from you. First, no one ever returned my call. Finally, I did manage to speak with someone. But, he told me that since my request was not a standard product, he did not have the time to help me. So, I went to your competitor.

As a customer, I have had it happen to me on several occasions. My response is usually:

> Wait, you do not understand. I am a potential customer. I want to talk to you about a way that I can give you money.

I know. I know. Sometimes you can get stuck on a wild goose chase. But, as discussed above, most good companies with a legitimate idea will share development expenses when the project is important to them. Being open to these new ideas is crucial. You already have a customer with a problem that is looking to you to help them find a solution. What could be better?

> One market area that brought in about $4M in annual sales in each of the last three years came from a phone call after the buyer found our name through a Google search. We then worked with the buyer to refine and develop a product that satisfied his requirements. In addition, one entrepreneur that I have worked with has built a successful $10M business just by responding aggressively to all inquiries and realizing that "you can always say 'no' later."

5. Actively Pursue New Product and Market Opportunities

For those businesses that have the size to support a new market and product development person, I would recommend that you hire one. Yes, I can hear you say:

> Wait a minute! Did you not just explain how you spent more than a million dollars and countless time and energy on new market and product development only to end up with $2M in annual sales.

Yes, I did. Nevertheless, if I had to do it over, I would still have a dedicated new product and market development person. First, markets are changing so rapidly that it is prudent to have one person dedicated to looking outward and immersed in new ideas and possibilities. The sales manager or marketing manager will have the best of intentions to spend time trying to look for new product and market opportunities. But this will always remain a lower priority as they quite rightly focus on satisfying current customers and increasing brand presence and share in current and related markets. Second, the market and product development person brings new ideas and vision that might be missed as the rest of us continue to look at the trees rather than the forest. In my case, our new product development influenced some of our other product offerings and marketing approaches. Third, while the new market development initiative did not pay off for us, I know of numerous cases where this initiative did hit the jackpot in finding an untapped need in a growing and profitable niche.

In short, consider your new market and product development as an investment option on a possible future direction of the business. It is another one-way bet. You will at most lose a little bit of money each year; but, if you win, the payoff could be huge.

To succeed with your new market and product development initiatives, you should:

1. Seek out Growing and Profitable Markets

2. Solve a Customer's Problems

3. Focus Where You Have a Competitive Advantage

• *Seek out Growing and Profitable Markets*
One of the key characteristics of successful new business development is to focus on the right markets in which to profitably grow your business. As Philip Delves Broughton said:

> The first challenge in strategy is picking the right thing to do. Pick the right industry, one with a sound structure, where your chances of making a profit are highest. This is where good strategy begins.

So, what defines the right market or right industry?

Growth

A growing market presents tremendous promise. By its very nature, the profit opportunity will continue to become larger and larger. Competitive pressure is usually less as there is less likely to be overcapacity. Further, the companies in the growing market are usually under pressure to deliver. As such, they are more open to assistance and partnership from suppliers that can help them deliver.

Size

You need to seek out industries or market niches that are large enough or have the potential to become large enough to be worth the time and effort to enter the market. A market niche that will never get larger than $2M may not be all that fruitful for an $80M business unit, especially if it requires a lot of change or customization to enter into.

Profitable

It is crucial to look at industries that are profitable. When evaluating an industry that has growth potential, first consider whether companies are making profit in that industry. Unless there is some special reason why an industry is temporarily unprofitable, marketplaces that are unprofitable usually stay unprofitable. Consider the domestic airline industry. Despite billions of dollars in investment, countless new entrants, numerous exits, constant shifts in strategy by major players, the industry has remained unprofitable for decades.

> *"When a management with a reputation for brilliance tackles a business with a reputation for bad economics, it is the reputation of the business that remains intact."*
>
> **Warren Buffett**

In trying to understand the profitability or potential profitability of a market or industry, consider performing a competitive dynamics evaluation using the well- known "Five Forces" model from Michael Porter.

Porter's Five Forces

1. What is the nature of the **competitive rivalry** in the industry? What is the overall profit level? How aggressive are the competitors?

2. What is the **threat of new competitors** entering the market? Are there barriers to entry making it difficult or costly for others to enter the industry? Are there barriers to exit that make it unlikely that incumbent competitors will ever leave the industry?

3. What is the nature and utility of alternative solutions to the products and services you provide? Are there **substitute products** in the industry that you have to compete against as well?

4. What is the **bargaining power of the customers**? Are there just a few, large and powerful customers?

5. What is the **bargaining power of the suppliers**? Are there are a few dominant suppliers who control key components of the product or services? Will you be able to offer enough value add to deflect any supplier power?

Although this looks a lot of detailed analysis, think 80 / 20 and devote just a few hours to analyze and discuss the competitive dynamics of the industries you are investigating. This time will be well spent if it helps you avoid committing resources into penetrating an unattractive industry or market niche.

Finding the Market

So, how do you go about finding that large, growing, profitable market or industry niche?

That is a simple question that is devilishly hard to answer. As I mentioned in my example, we spent years trying to find the perfect niche with only modest success. In their insight book *Blue Ocean Strategy*, W. Chan

> *The concept of Blue Ocean is defined by untapped market space, differentiation, and the opportunity for highly profitable growth without all the competitors. Consider products and businesses such as Cirque De Soleil, Chrysler Minivan, CNN, Body Shop, Southwest and Ryanair.*
> *Blue Ocean Strategy*

Kim and Renée Mauborgne discuss finding new markets and building sustainable and profitable business models. Their thesis is that most companies focus on beating the competition in the bloody red ocean where all the fish and predators are swimming around and eating one another. Instead, winning businesses should focus on finding and creating unique value in untapped market spaces where no one else is competing – the blue ocean.

Naturally, finding a blue ocean is ideal. It is also difficult. In putting together a brief list of the fundamentals, I combine ideas from *Blue Ocean Strategy* with my own experience to give you five places to start looking.

1. **Look at other industries which your suppliers sell to.**

2. **Look at other industries that companies in the chain of purchasing sell to.** What other industries does your customer sell to? What industries are the end users (those who actually use the product) in? What other industries are influencers (consultants, advisors, specifiers, etc.) involved in?

3. **Look across complementary product and service offerings.** What happens before, during and after your product is used? What is the context in which your product is used? What are the pain points? How can they be eliminated through a complementary product and service offering?

4. **Look across alternative industries that you may compete with indirectly.**

5. **Look across time.** What are the mega-trends and demographic trends that are decisive, irreversible, and with a clear trajectory. As an example, today you might consider the rise of China and emerging markets and the number of baby boomers retiring as such trends.

Again, this seems like a lot. But, spending a little bit of time talking to your suppliers, customers, end users, and influencers will not only improve these relationships. It will go a long way towards identifying potential markets for further research and analysis.

- *Solve a Customer's Problems*

No customer has ever bought anything because it was "strategically logical" or "synergistic."A customer buys from you because he has a problem, and he needs you to help solve his problem. Far too often business leaders have a great product or great technology that is just a solution looking for a problem.

> In 2006, our parent company acquired a competitor that had a standardized product line. I was tasked to grow and develop this product line. By being standardized, this particular product line appeared to be logical for a national company to buy. The products that the customers would buy would be the same whether they bought them in San Diego or in Philadelphia. Further, the customers could standardize their installation and maintenance of the product.

> There was just one problem. The customers did not want a standardized product line. The purchasing decisions were made at the local and regional level and the local people did not want anything to do with this new product. All of their installation and maintenance crews were familiar with the more specialized products that that region already bought. Further, a standardized product would take power out of local hands and give it to the national corporate entity, jeopardizing local and regional jobs.

> But, we had a great solution. So, my team and I soldiered on for two years and nearly $1.5M before shutting the business down; beating your head against the wall only feels good when you stop. We had it exactly backward. We had a solution looking for a problem that the customer

> *"Creating demand, even with a great product, is hard. Filling demand is much easier. Don't create a product, then seek to have someone see its potential. Find a market — define your customers — then find or develop a product for them."*
>
> **Tim Ferriss**

did not seem to think was a problem. And further, even if it was a problem, the customer had their own reasons for not wanting it to be solved in the way we proposed.

As always, the customer is only concerned about what is in it for them. How can the supplier help the customer to make his business better?

As my colleague Martin Zwilling advises:

Don't make the mistake of looking at market needs or requests as an afterthought to verify what's already been planned.

Go out first and talk with potential customers, listening to their problems and hearing about their pain points. Then focus on solving these problems and soothing their pain. Once you have done that, your new product or market development initiative will have potential.

* *Focus Where You Have a Competitive Advantage*

In *Blue Ocean Strategy*, the authors stress the need to create such a leap in value that only your company with its unique capabilities can satisfy the market need. As such, you are competing with a huge and sustainable competitive advantage, and the competition becomes less relevant.

The most familiar example might be the initial Southwest Airlines business model with its focus on tremendous uniformity (exact same planes and procedures), its quick turn-around (no assigned seating), its frequent and short flights, and its low fares. With all that, they created a business model that was nearly impossible for another airline to replicate.

Creating such a sustained competitive advantage requires that your company is aligned so that what you deliver to the marketplace cannot be easily copied by anyone else. You are able to differentiate your market offering and deliver it with an efficiency that no one else can duplicate. In this case, Southwest delivers frequent, low fare flights that differentiate it from everyone else. With their uniformity and quick turn-around, they deliver it more efficiently than anyone else can.

So, how do you find that market niche where your competitive advantage is sustainable?

Know Your Competition

The first step is a candid analysis of how your business matches up with the competition or potential competition.

- What are your company's relative strengths and weaknesses? What are your competitors' relative strengths and weaknesses?
- What are the differences in equipment and production systems?
- What are the differences in products and product range?
- What are the differences in corporate cultures? Engineering or production culture? Sales and marketing culture?
- Does location matter? If so, who has a location advantage or disadvantage?
- Does anyone have specialized knowledge that others do not?
- Who has better and stronger customer and personal relations with key customers?
- What are the relative financial strength and stability of the companies?

> *"For business strategy, you want to focus on competitive advantage. But, take it one step further. You want to focus on not going where you have a competitive disadvantage."*
>
> **Phillip Delves Boughton**

The hardest part of this analysis is being candid and humble. Most companies think that they are superior to their competitors on all levels. To do this analysis effectively, you need to get beyond the pride and ego and realize that your competitors do some things better than you do.

Once you have assembled your list of strengths and weaknesses. Compare them to the market that you are considering entering:

- How much does each strength or weakness matter in the market?
- Are your relative strengths a fit to the market structure and dynamics? Or will you just be a "me too" supplier?
- Can your competitive weaknesses be overcome?
- How else can you differentiate yourself?
- Can your competitive advantage be sustained?

Consider the Success Scenario

In considering your competitive positioning, it often helps to "play it forward" with different scenarios, especially the success scenario. In the success scenario, you assume that your business has been successful at entering the market and establishing a good competitive position. Now, brainstorm about what this future state looks like and what are the consequences of this success.

- What will your company be required to deliver? **How will you be organized to deliver on the differentiation more efficiently than the competition?** Do you have the people capable of delivering on this promise effectively?
- **Will you be able to sustain your differentiation and the competitive advantage?** Or will you just raise the cost of doing business for all supplier companies without differentiating yourself?
- **Will you be competing against your current customers or current key suppliers?**

If we had worked through a success scenario on the standardized product line discussed earlier, we would have come up with some challenges. First, we would have satisfied the corporate staff of our incumbent national customers, but alienated the local and regional teams who had all the power day to day on the ground. Second, we would have lowered the barriers to entry in the market since one crucial barrier is that the tooling required for the specialized products differed from customer to customer. As a result, we would have opened the door to smaller, more aggressive, but financially weaker competitors who had until now been excluded from the market. In short, not considering the Success Scenario cost us the considerable time and money spent on this failed initiative.

To repeat, your competitive advantage will only be sustainable when your company and its mix of structure, abilities, and people is the best company to deliver effectively and efficiently on what the customers in that market want. In such a case, you will be playing to your strengths and against your competitor's weaknesses.

Time Out: I can hear you saying it once again. Too much work. Too much theory. Too much thinking. Analysis Paralysis. Yes, it can become that. As always, short strategy sessions where 80% of the critical thought can be done in 20% of the time are essential. As I have learned from my experience with the standardized product line, rigorous thinking before action saves time, money and heartbreak.

Focus Focus Focus.

Face reality: your company can only be the best in the world and have a significant competitive advantage in a few markets. As such, the biggest

> *"A company is more likely to die of indigestion from too much opportunity than starvation from too little."*
> *David Packard (Co-founder of HP)*

challenge in strategy will be to focus relentlessly on only those few areas. As I have stressed before, creating this focus requires making a conscious decision to not do something. And, at times, it can even mean saying 'No' to a good and loyal customer. Nonetheless, the fundamental of strategy and business development remains unchanged: focus on less in order to do what you do better.

But, What about Acquisitions?

Acquisitions can be effective tools to speed the growth and development of your business. Through acquisitions your business can expand into new geographic areas, enter new market spaces, broaden product lines, develop relationships with new and growing customers, and bring in new and useful technologies. And, yes, acquisitions can be used to buy out pesky competitors, thus eliminating them from "screwing up" your market.

A detailed discussion of acquisitions is beyond the scope of this book. Nevertheless, I will give a few thoughts about the role of acquisitions in growing your business.

First, realize that all acquisitions are risky and difficult. Countless surveys estimate the success rate on acquisitions at less than 50%[18]. By paying in cash or stock up front, acquisitions are big, bold bets on the future that often do not pan out and can fail spectacularly. Further, acquisition integration is hard. Bringing together two different corporate cultures and two diverse ways of doing business takes a lot of management time and effort that can distract the leader from the rest of the business. To reduce this risk, you need to be sure that you have the strong leadership team to undertake the acquisition.

Second, acquire a company for the right reason. Acquisitions, like initiatives, are sometimes used to mask the weakness in accountability and execution in the current business. If you are not currently successful or growing, do not consider acquisitions as a viable strategy to help save your company from its current under-performance. Fix your own business first.

Third, ensure that the acquisition fits with your business development goals like a glove. As such, the acquisition has to bring something unique and useful: strong relations with additional

---

18   Each survey usually comes up with a different number for the success rate of acquisitions. The numbers that I have seen most often are between 40% and 45%.

customers in your market space, new products or production technologies for your market space, or a strong presence in a closely related and growing market space. In general, it is best to pay a little more and buy a strong, viable, even dominant, business.

Finally, if you want to consider acquisitions, then have an acquisition strategy. Target the companies that you would like to acquire over the next one to three years and begin to make contacts and build relationships now. This will ensure that your company will be the one getting the call when the target decides to sell. In the best case, you may be able to negotiate with the target directly without other potential buyers being involved.

> The most successful acquisitions that my team completed had been on our acquisition target list for years. In one typical case, we targeted the company starting in 1998, looked to do a joint venture with them in 1999, continued to keep in touch over the intervening years, and finally acquired them in late 2002. When the time came, they reached out to us, and we were ready to move quickly. It is true that they had also considered other potential buyers; but there was no auction or bidding war so we got the deal done at the right price.

Yes, the opportunistic deal may fall in your company's lap. But, it is far more likely that if you do not develop relationships with prospective acquisition targets that a competitor or Private Equity buyer will contact the target at the right time. The company will then either sell without your knowledge, or the company will put itself up for auction requiring you to pay top dollar.

SECTION VI – CONCLUSION

CHAPTER 26 –
WRAP-UP

"The Main Thing is to Keep the Main Thing the Main Thing"

German Proverb

Well, that is all that there is.

I know. I know. There are many important topics that I have omitted or discussed only briefly:

- Sales, marketing and branding
- Production and operations
- Acquisitions
- Quality
- Safety
- Information technology
- Finance
- Work-life balance

It has been difficult for me to say 'No' and omit many of these topics. But, I have worked hard to keep this book short, simple and focused, largely because the theme of this book is to keep things short, simple and focused.

To wrap-up, the "Main Thing" of this book has been the contention that business leaders can realize greater success by fixating on three fundamentals:

1. **Do the Right Thing.** Build an ethical organization aligned to tackle the critical issues.

2. **Winning Teamwork.** Create an engaged and accountable team that executes on the business goals.

3. **Customer Service.** Develop a customer service culture that exceeds the expectations of current customers and allows for profitable growth.

There may be no great insight in these three fundamentals. But, a quick scan around the business world suggests that these fundamentals have often been forgotten.

- Ethical violations abound at the highest level with a distinct lack of leadership and accountability at all levels.
- Companies and individuals are overwhelmed and pulled in far too many directions with too much information and too many priorities.
- Employee engagement and motivation are at record lows, all but ensuring a lack of alignment between the goals of the leadership and the daily goals and activities of the employee.
- Customer service remains a rarity in all but a prosperous handful of companies.
- In our slow-growth economy the limited opportunities for profitable growth are not being realized.

Dedicating yourself as a leader to these three fundamentals will help you to make your people more successful. In turn, this will make your business more successful, which will make you personally more successful.

CHAPTER 27 –
FINAL EXAM

"Perhaps the most valuable result of all education and learning is the ability to make yourself do the thing that you have to do, when it ought to be done, whether you like it or not; it is the first lesson that ought to be learned."

Thomas Huxley (English biologist)

"Knowing is not enough; we must apply.
Willing is not enough; we must do."

Johann Wolfgang Von Goethe

For those of you who have stayed with me to the very end, I want to say: "Thank You." I appreciate your interest and hope that you consider the time we have spent together to be time well spent.

It is now time for me to pass the baton on to you. My role, at least for the time being, is done. It is your time to roll up your sleeves and get to work. It is your turn to take that dreaded final exam. And it is your opportunity to take the ideas that we have discussed here and apply and do them in your business.

I sincerely wish you the best of luck and the best of success with your business (yeah sure, even my current and future competitors).

You can keep up with what I am doing at my blog on Winning B2B Leadership[SM] at www.winningB2Bleadership.com. I look forward to responding to your thoughts, feed-back, and suggestions. And I look forward to hearing your insightful quotes, additional examples and anecdotes.

Final Exam

1. What are the three fundamentals of leading your winning business that require your uncompromising daily focus?

2. To build and improve your business, what three things do you intend to make yourself do, whether you want to do them or not?

BIBLIOGRAPHY

Abrashoff, Michael. *It's Your Ship: Management Techniques from the Best Damn Ship in the Navy.* Business Plus. 2002.

Blanchard, Kenneth H, and Sheldon Bowles. *Raving Fans: A Revolutionary Approach to Customer Service.* William Morrow. 1993.

_____, Patricia Zigarmi, and Drea Zigarmi. *Leadership and the One Minute Manager: Increasing Effectiveness by Being a Good Leader.* HarperCollins Entertainment. 2000.

_____. *Leading at a Higher Level: Blanchard on Leadership and Creating High Performance Organizations.* FT Press. 2009.

Bossidy, Larry and Ram Charan. *Execution: The Discipline of Getting Things Done.* Crown Business. 2002.

Bradt, George B., Jayme A. Check, Jorge E. Pedraza. *The New Leader's 100-Day Action Plan.* John Wiley & Sons, Inc.: Hoboken, New Jersey. 2009

Broughton, Philip Delves. *Ahead of the Curve: Two Years at Harvard Business School.* PenguinPress HC. 2008.

Charan, Ram, Steve Drotter and Jim Noel. *The Leadership Pipeline: How to Build the Leadership Powered Company.* Jossey-Bass. 2000.

Collins, Jim. *Good to Great: Why Some Companies Make the Leap. . .and Others Don't.* Harper Business. 2001.

_____. *How the Mighty Fall: And Why Some Companies Never Give In.* Jim Collins. 2009.

Connors, Roger, Tom Smith and Craig Hickman. *The Oz Principle: Getting Results Through Individual and Corporate Accountability.* Portfolio Hardcover. 2004.

Covey, Stephen R. *The Seven Habits of Highly Effective People: Powerful Lessons in Personal Change.* Free Press. 2004

_____.*The 8th Habit: From Effectiveness to Greatness.* Free Press. 2005.

Drucker, Peter. *The Essential Drucker: The Best of Sixty Years of Peter Drucker's Essential Writing on Management.* HarperBusiness. 2001.

Ferriss, Timothy. *The 4-Hour Workweek.* Crown Publishers: New York. 2009.

Gadiesh, Orit, and Hugh MacArthur. *Lessons from Private Equity Any Company Can Use.* Harvard Business Press: Boston.2008.

Gerstner Jr., Louis V. *Who Says Elephants Can't Dance – How I Turned Around IBM.* Harper Collins Publishers Ltd. 2003.

Goldratt, Eliyahu M and Jeff Cox. *The Goal: A Process of Ongoing Improvement.* North River Press. 2004.

Goldsmith, Marshall. *What Got You Here Won't Get You There: How Successful People Become Even More Successful.* Hyperion. 2007.

Hammer, Michael. *The Agenda: What Every Business Must Do to Dominate the Decade.* Three Rivers Press. 2003.

Harford, Tim. *The Logic of Life: The Rational Economics of an Irrational World.* Random House Trade Paperbacks. 2009.

Heath, Chip and Dan Heath. *Made to Stick: Why Some Ideas Survive and Others Die.* Random House. 2007.

_____ and Dan Heath. *Switch: How to Change When Change is Hard.* Crown Business. 2010.

Kim, Chan W. and Renée Mauborgne. *Blue Ocean Strategy: How to Create Uncontested Market Space and Make Competition Irrelevant.* Harvard Business Press. 2005.

Laffer, Arthur B., William J. Hass and Shepherd G. Pryor IV. *The Private Equity Edge: How Private Equity Players and the World's Top Companies Build Value and Wealth.* McGraw-Hill: New York. 2009.

Lombardo, Michael M. and Robert W. Eichinger. *The Leadership Machine: Architecture to Develop Leaders for any Future.* Lominger International. 2006.

Porter, Michael E. *Competitive Strategy: Techniques for Analyzing Industries and Competitors.* Free Press. 1998.

Rackham, Neil. *Spin Selling.* McGraw-Hill. 1988.

Rasiel, Ethan M. *The McKinsey Way: Using the Techniques of the World's Top Strategic Consultants to Help You and Your Business.* McGraw-Hill. 1999.

Soundview Editorial Staff, Eds. *Skills for Success: The Experts Show the Way.* Soundview Executive Book Summaries. 1988.

Stewart, Matthew. *The Management Myth: Debunking Modern Business Philosophy.* W.W. Norton & Company. 2010.

Welch, Jack with John A. Byrne. *Jack: Straight from the Gut.* Business Plus. 2003.

_____ and Suzy Welch. *Winning.* Harper Business. 2005

Zwilling, Martin. *Do You Have What It Takes to Be an Entrepreneur?* Ingram Publisher Services. 2010.

Index

8056341R0

Made in the USA
Charleston, SC
04 May 2011